Ramesh,

EXCESS RETURNS

May all of your
real estate investments
bring you double
digit returns!

May all of your

EXCESS RETURNS

Exploiting the Inefficiencies in Today's Real
Estate Market with Lease 2 Owns

Greg Hughes

ISBN: 978-0-9849608-8-0

Printed in the United States of America.

This publication is designed to provide accurate and authoritative information in regard to the subject matter covered. It is sold with the understanding that the publisher is not engaged in rendering legal, accounting or other professional services. If legal advice or other expert assistance is required, the services of a competent professional person should be sought.

Greg Hughes
Hughes Private Capital, LLC
My Lease 2 Own, LLC
5440 Louie Lane Suite 106
Reno, NV 89511

(775) 297-4977
Greg@HughesCapital.com
www.HughesCapital.com
www.MyLease2Own.com

TABLE OF CONTENTS

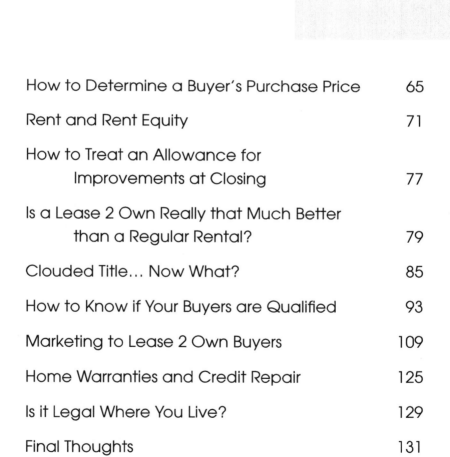

AN ADULT FAIRY TALE

*T*he land below his feet was plentiful with rich soil that
was willing to grow anything his heart desired in great
abundance; yet the poor farmer stood there with nothing but
dust swirling around his head. Thoughts of how to provide for
his family beat down on him, like the relentless sun, day in and
day out.

Each year that passed had only become worse. He wasn't
afraid of working hard. He didn't expect to get rich overnight.
He wasn't one to ever complain and didn't need anyone to hold
his hand like those others who expected someone to give them
something for nothing.

At one time his farm had flourished, but over the last few
years he was slowly not being able to provide for his family as
well as he had before. Yet, nothing had changed with his farm's
soil or his hard work ethic and he was working harder now than
ever before.

Many times his government representatives (there were so many it was hard to keep track of them) had visited his farm in order to "help out," while simultaneously looking out for the best interest of all farmers. They would tell him things like when he could water, what types of rakes to use, and how tall to grow his crops. The most disturbing change was when they decreed that his four kids could no longer help out during weekends on the farm. The unions thought it was essential that kids have their play time prior to going back to school on Monday... and the government agreed.

Out of every crop, he was now required to give more to the newly formed government agency entitled the "Board of Liberal Looting, Sharing, Helping in Trade," which was more commonly known as BoLLSHiT.

He had always been generous before when a neighbor, friend, family member, or even a stranger needed help, but now he doesn't really have that choice. His government representative instructed that it is best just to let BoLLSHit divvy up his crop share, in the fairest way for all involved and they said they know best.

The farmer's Mom and Dad had taught him to share and now he was trying to teach his kids the same. However, that was hard with the new law stating that kids are only required to listen to their parents for 15 minutes per day. He was told that everyone in the country thought kids shouldn't be "brain-washed" excessively by parents. This "brainwashing" might lead them to a lack of understanding on how the new world works and why so many others unfairly don't have the same size farm as them, if at all.

It was a tough new world, yet his gut told him that the riches he had before and the riches others have been able to earn are still there, but perhaps more hidden than usual. How could he find those riches again?

One day the farmer stumbled across something that his help-ful government representatives had not joyously regulated into oblivion. It seemed like a golden idea of how to help out others in this bleak and trying time.

He gathered up a few other farmers and told them of his idea. If they were able to pool their money together and help others to get back into their own farm, maybe everyone could emerge as winners.

He worked feverishly on it day and night. Finally, after thou-sands of hours of unbroken toil, he found what he crowned a "Lease 2 Own." He discovered that by treating those other farmers who were caught in turmoil with the respect they deserved, they were very interested in having their own farms again. There, they could rebuild their lives through hard work and have prosperity within their reach once more.

In return, they were willing to pay a little extra as thanks to all of the farmer's friends and family that helped them to get their new farms. In the most dismal of times was born the grandest of ideas. Let one farmer help another farmer out...

... And everyone lives happily ever after. I bet you don't remember your parents reading that story to you when you were a little kid. Now our adult fairy tale ends and the rest of the story begins. Please enjoy.

Greg Hogan

## CHAPTER 1

WHY ME AND WHO CARES?

W hen I first sat down to write this book I had to ask, "Why me and who cares?" I continued to ask that of myself as I wrote for hours on end. Why would anyone bother to read a word I put down on paper?

Part of the answer is because I know this is not going to be some *New York Times* bestseller or going to be acknowledged by Oprah, but that is not why I want to write this book. I wanted to write to share my involvement in real estate with other real estate Investors. I want to inform Investors of all my ups and downs, things that worked and things that didn't, the minor items that you have no idea will present themselves until they do and how to handle or avoid them. These are the hard things to learn that really only come with doing something day in and day out over and over again. They call that experience.

From that experience comes my true and passionate interest in sharing with you what I have learned, in order for you to be able to successfully invest in real estate and avoid all the "experience" that I had to go through.

Investing in real estate is not rocket science. If a guy that used to mow lawns for a living and has never graduated from college can be wildly successful at it, so can you! My passion is to share what I have learned and show you the methods that work every time with consistent results.

In fact, what's interesting is that if you do it the right way you can literally build a real estate empire with almost no downside risk.

Now think of that last statement. No downside risk? Don't all investments have a downside risk? Yes, and ok, so does our real estate investment strategy. However, if done correctly, the downside risk or even a negative cash flow is almost nil, zip, zero, nada. I like to say with our system you get, "the safety of a savings account with lucrative returns."

I was having lunch the other day with one of my super successful and affluent friends and she astounded me with one of her comments. She said she doesn't even like to open her investment statements when she gets them in the mail.

She told me about how she would get them in the mail, put them on her desk at home and walk past them over and over without opening them. She didn't open them because if her investments had gone down that month it made her almost sick to her stomach. Then she said she would finally have to open them because she was so curious, despite finding herself disappointed again and again

"YOU REALLY HAVEN'T LOST
ANY MONEY...YOUR ACCOUNT
IS JUST WORTH LESS NOW."

when there were down months. She even went as far as to tell her financial advisor to only send them quarterly.

Now, here is a very sophisticated and wealthy businesswoman that hates opening her investment statements. I don't think she is alone with those feelings about her investments. Making and managing investment decisions is usually a painful process for most people.

Just look at how my friend handles her investment and management decisions compared to her business decisions. She will make extremely quick, high dollar decisions for her business all day long and not blink an eye. Yet, when it comes to just opening her investment statements that are professionally managed, you would think someone asked her to crawl along the floor on her hands and knees across broken glass.

What happens if instead, you were able to open your investment statements and always know that it was going up? Then my friend wouldn't have to play those mental games with herself. That is exactly what I propose to show you and how to do it anywhere you live and in any kind of market.

## CHAPTER 2

PLAN B – HOW TO PROTECT YOUR DOWNSIDE RISK

*L*et's expand on how to protect yourself from downside risk. Most of the time, here at Hughes Private Capital, we are able to create 10% to 20% returns on our real estate investments very consistently over and over again.

However, they don't all work out exactly as planned. That's okay. We can't win them all, but what we *can* do is position ourselves correctly so that when it doesn't work out exactly as planned, we have a back-up plan, "Plan B," to protect our investment.

I'm going to show you how to do that and maybe it will only increase your return from 5% to 10%, but my guess is that you can live with that kind of return. I know many people that are down-right giddy with what we consider our "low return" Plan B.

Before we get started, let's define what "Plan B" is for our discussion. Plan B is our back up plan. When an investment doesn't go exactly as planned at any time in its duration, then what is your Plan B? First, do you have one and second, what is it? In our case, you will learn later in the book, our Plan B is a solid rentable property with a positive cash flow.

The point is that a lower Plan B return can be and should be on the positive side, so your investments are never going backward, but actually just moving forward more slowly. Once you are able to achieve it, this type of investment almost guarantees a return and peace of mind can be yours…at least for that investment!

Read that last paragraph again. It is possibly the most important reason to follow my program and especially if you are risk averse. With the proper Plan B in place, your risk of loss should almost be completely eliminated.

Normally, eliminating your downsize risk usually translates into very low returns in the very low single digits. This is where I am going to show you how we developed a program that takes advantage of what we call "Excess Returns" in the real estate market.

Excess Returns are what is known in investing terms as an Alpha. An Alpha is defined in this case as being the spread between your upside return on investment compared to the commensurate, or expected downside risk, for that return. That spread is then usually benchmarked against other similar investments to compare the amount of potential risk to the potential return. The wider you can manage that spread the better. I.E., the highest amount of return with the lowest amount of risk; back to "the safety of a savings account with lucrative returns."

The great oracle of Omaha, Warren Buffett, said in his letter to shareholders, **"Housing will come back – you can be sure of that."** Then he went to exclaim on CNBC Squawk Box, **"I would buy a couple hundred thousand homes, if I could."**

What Mr. Buffett recognizes are these inefficiencies. He knows the spread between the return and risk, or the alpha, is leaning heavily on the "investment scale" towards the Investors' favor right now. Anytime you can find an investment that has a large alpha, which creates excess returns, you are able to get a far superior return for a minimal amount of risk. This is how Investors get rich.

A quick example is a Certificate of Deposit (CD) in a bank. While CDs are usually extremely safe with almost no downside risk to speak of (other than inflation), the return on investment is miniscule: Very low single digit returns, sometimes even less than 1%, depending on the fiscal policies of the Feds at the time.

Great! It is a safe investment, but you'll get almost no return on your money and *literally*, if inflation is greater than the return you are receiving on that bank CD, then your money is losing buying power daily. It would then be a Certificate of Disappointment (CD).

What would happen if you could take that same extremely low chance of downsize risk yet give it a return of 6%, 8%, or even in the double digits? Then, my friend, you would have what is known

CERTIFICATE OF DISAPPOINTMENT

as excess return: your spread being greater between the return on your investment compared to your downside risk.

Just make sure the spread is in the right direction, because it can be the opposite and give you more downside risk than appropriate for the return on investment.

Finding excess return in any kind of investment is the way Investors get rich. It is done all day long on Wall Street with the people in the know. Now I am going to be able to show you how to take advantage of the excess return. I discovered and developed it over thousands of hours of tweaking, changing, putting it back together, evolving, working with real estate agents, attorneys, accountants, Buyers, Investors, etc. to be able to exploit it to produce consistent double digit returns with a very minimized downsized risk.

The best way to get started is with a story about how my company got to where it is today. Like most companies, it slowly evolved and morphed into what it currently is and it definitely did not just happen overnight. Along the way there was a lot of worrying. We repeatedly questioned ourselves if we were doing things the right way and we made mistakes which we learned from in order for us to do it correctly the next time. Isn't it always that way in life?

I want to shorten the time frame for you by helping you to avoid the plentiful mistakes that we made. Without those mistakes slowing you down, you will enjoy a less painful road to raise your investments to the point we are at today with the amount of success we have.

I started investing in real estate at the ripe old age of 19. I found a property in a run-down neighborhood where most of the buildings were either rentals or commercial buildings.

THIS WAS MY FIRST PURCHASE AT 19 YEARS OLD. IT
HAD THREE HOMES ON ONE LOT, IN WHICH I RENTED
TWO OF THEM OUT AND LIVED IN THE THIRD.

The property was located across the street from my stepfather's office and was somewhat isolated from the rest of the neighborhood. On it, sat three white and green houses, all very small with one or two bedrooms in each, stucco exteriors, composite roofs, and one small garage that a car wouldn't even fit in. It was more of a shed disguised as a garage with an old pull up door. These houses sat on a non-picturesque half-acre and believe it or not, had a white picket fence out front to complete the picture (though, the fence wasn't all standing straight up).

Needless to say, I was confident these 50-60 year old homes were not about to win any Home and Garden awards. The man that owned them lived in the back house. He was 72 years old and had been a widower for some time. He had a small Schnauzer named Taffy and the dog actually ate taffy out of his hand all day long. Why? I don't know. He had been trying to sell the property for some time now, but he was old and grumpy and kept running off the real estate agents that wanted to sell it for him.

I kept looking at this property whenever I visited my stepfather's office and knew it would be perfect for me and my business at the time. I had a small lawn mowing business that I had started when I was 15 years old and had continued with it, since I made good money, while I attended college.

I finally got up the guts to talk to this man about what he wanted to do with his property. I walked over there, scared from all the previous stories I had heard about him and knocked on the door. I told him I was interested in talking to him about his property. Low and behold, he invited me in.

It was going okay so far. I sat on his couch in his small living room while he sat across from me in his chair. He proceeded to feed his dog a piece of taffy every so often. He would click the taffy on the arm of his chair and without a moment's hesitation; this overweight Schnauzer would come waddling in to get his piece of taffy. Have you ever seen a dog eat taffy? It's like when they have peanut butter stuck to the roof of their mouth and are working their hardest to get it off. Why a regular dog bone wouldn't suffice, I don't know, maybe because he would have to name him Dog Bone?

Anyway, I proceeded to sit and talk with him many times for many hours over the next few weeks and I figured out that this grumpy old man really just wanted someone to talk to. He had been alone for a long time since his wife died. That was a big lesson for me. Sometimes the slower path is faster in the end. If I would have just rushed right in there and never taken the time that I spent with him, I probably would have never been able to buy the property.

We worked out a deal where he carried the paper for me, I put down a decent deposit and he got to move up to Seattle to, as he would say, "watch the ships come and go." I moved into his house and kept the two renters in the front two houses and owned my first property.

I am sure you remember the first home that you owned. You probably have some fond memories even if everything wasn't perfect. You loved it because it was yours. My fondest memory was being amazed that the little junky garage was all mine and how great that felt. I didn't have to share it with my parents or sister and I could do whatever I wanted. I had hit the big time at 19, or so I told myself.

Initially, the garage was an absolute disaster since the old man had had his dryer out in the garage, but never bothered to vent out the lint. The lint literally covered the whole garage like snow, but it didn't matter to me because it was *my* garage.

## CHAPTER 3

JUST THE FACTS, MA'AM

*R*emember the old show, *"Dragnet,"* with Jack Webb who played Sargent Joe Friday, and who used to say, "Just the facts, ma'am?"

YOU CAN HEAR THE THEME SONG NOW IN YOUR HEAD AS SOME OF THOSE MEMORIES COME BACK. (DUM..DE..DUM..DUM)

Maybe Sargent Joe Friday was out for just the facts, but what I have found is that while Investors start out looking for the facts, that is not really what they are looking for.

None of us invest because we are going to receive 12.1495% return on our investment. That return can only represent something else to us. We seek investments as if that is the end result, but that is like saying we buy a car to get from point A to point B. That may be the initial need, but there is so much more to the decision when we buy or invest.

In this book, I am for the most part going to only deal with "the facts, ma'am" interspersed with ideas and stories that have infiltrated my investing career. I do however want to address before we get too far into the book what I consider the "Independence Factor."

I can tell you from working with hundreds of Investors, right now there is not one person reading this book who is not striving for financial independence or is not interested in maintaining their financial independence. Those individuals who don't care about bettering themselves are not reading this book.

You are, of course, reading this book and really when you boil down to all the reasons why, it is for financial independence. That is the only reason you ever invest.

What financial independence looks like for each individual Investor is definitely not the same for everyone. It can have wide variations, yet it is probably similar in more ways than different.

I want to boil it down to one statement that should fit all. The "Independence Factor" means the ability to do what you want, when you want, with whom you want, how you want and just because you want to. Would you agree with me, that sums it all up? As Investors, we want to be able to have it all, as we want it.

For you that may be living the life you want in retirement, to taking the family on a vacation, to buying a second or third home, to not stressing over the economy, to leaving something for your family when you are gone, to not hearing your boss or employees whine for one more day, to being in complete control of your life every day from this point forward.

Let's not lose track as to why we do what we do. It also never ends even once we have achieved that financial independence because we then have to maintain it and no one likes to go backwards.

So why bring all this up? I want you to be in the right frame of mind as you learn throughout the rest of this book about my secrets and systems of how to achieve exactly that financial independence. Yes, it is great to have lucrative returns and minimal risk, but what is most important are your long term goals and aspirations.

Whatever those goals and aspirations look like today and no matter how good any investment looks or sounds, don't stick all of your eggs into one basket, even if it does work for the Easter Bunny. Remember to diversify and spread your risk. Yes, at times you can heavily lean toward one or a few investments, but don't bet it all on just one or two.

We all want to invest in things that seem to at least be for the good of all involved. In other words, we really don't want to invest

"THE 'PUT ALL YOUR EGGS IN
ONE BASKET STRATEGY'
SEEMS TO WORK FOR HIM."

in companies, stocks, businesses or people that will have a net negative effect for some of the parties involved. That is why I have been so excited for and such an advocate of our Lease 2 Own program.

In the end, all the parties win. No one party in the scenario is at a disadvantage. This includes our Lease 2 Own Buyers. They get a second shot at becoming financially independent and reaching their goals and aspirations. Those are just the facts, ma'am (sir).

## CHAPTER 4

OWNING YOUR OWN HOME AND THE AMERICAN DREAM

*A*fter owning your home for the first time, you never want to go back to renting and living in a place that isn't yours again. This is a big part of what we base our real estate philosophy on: Helping people get into their own home again or, for some, their first time.

In this win-win situation, everything we do has to benefit all who are involved or it doesn't work. To build a business, a reputation, and long-term equity in our real estate portfolio, *plus* have happy Investors and Buyers, out of the hundreds if not thousands of times we do a deal, it has to benefit everyone involved.

Let me skip ahead 19 years. After building my successful lawn and landscape business with $5 million in sales and over 100 employees, I sold the company to my partner that I had taken on in the last 4 years of owning the company. I took 3 ½ months off and traveled with my wife and four kids. We went to Hawaii, New Zealand and Australia. It was one of the greatest trips of my life. My four kids ranged from 4 to 10 years old at the time and I was able to spend quality time with them every day.

As a serial entrepreneur, I ran various businesses over the next few years. My businesses were of very different types. There was the incredibly forward-thinking and fun furniture store I opened up with a partner that ran it day to day. When I was in Sydney, Australia, I found a golf training product that I licensed in the United States. It was sold through home shows, the internet, pro-shops and at mall kiosks. It was a great product to demo. However, nothing really got my juices flowing like real estate and finance.

One of my friends was just starting to raise money as a business for developers through the use of 1st Trust Deeds for commercial projects. It sounded all very exciting to me and it combined real estate with finance.

So, I decided to join my friend in his business and I thought this was going to be the way to go. It was so much fun being able to take the real estate and marry it together with finance. In just a year and a half, we had raised $65 million. Unfortunately, what I didn't know was that the country's economy was going to melt down, and not just a little bit, but a lot.

Even with my furniture store, I was going to learn a hard lesson. When I first started working on my due diligence for the furniture store, I spent almost a year making sure it was going to be a viable business. I kept telling myself that if the furniture store didn't work out, I would be okay since I bought the building and owned commercial real estate. Again, I was too naïve to know that when one thing melts down, often everything melts down along with it.

This is exactly what we have all experienced in the past few years; no doubt some people more than others. I joke that I have a half-million dollar chair in my house that proves that point. When all was said and done, it was an expensive lesson without much more to show for it than a few pieces of furniture we kept at the end of closing down the store.

I still own the commercial building, but it's been difficult in getting it leased and making money on it. So much for the building I purchased being my fail-safe for my investment. Actually, my experience with that whole deal will have to be for another book and another time.

Now as for the 1st trust deeds, I was going to get another one of those lessons taught to me in a big way. I always believe that if you're going to ask someone else to invest in something, you should also be fully invested in it so you can put your money where your mouth is. That is, of course, what I did with the 1st trust deeds. These were mostly properties that were vacant land which were going to be used for developing some type of commercial projects and/or housing development projects.

I recognize today that vacant land is not worth that much when no one wants to buy it or build on it. Even premium lakefront lots that lie right on one of the most beautiful lakes in the world, Lake Tahoe, or 21.5 acres in one of the most prestigious ski resorts in the world, Squaw Valley, aren't worth anything with no Buyer to sell them to. I am now the proud owner of these properties and will have to wait for years before I can recover my money.

My investments have gone from being something that pays me every month to an out of pocket expense every month until the time they can be sold.

Here are the lessons you should take from these debacles:

1. They are not income producing properties (in fact, they are just the opposite).

2. They are all commercial properties.

How does all this tie together? What I have come to understand is non-income producing properties, no matter how attractive they may seem, are extremely risky. We talked about the downside earlier. You need to have someone interested in your property for it to have value. So what is Plan B? I thought with these non-income producing properties I was always covered because I was only loaning a small fraction of the value of the property and if I had to take it back then I could easily sell it for what was loaned on it. I was completely wrong in my assumptions. When things go bad, the vacant land/non-income producing properties are the first to go!

A great example of this is the 21.5 acres in Squaw Valley, CA.

This is absolutely prime land in a prime place and the last vacant land that is developable in Squaw Valley. It was appraised for $37 million without entitlements and our loan was for $11 million. You would think the worst case scenario would be that it could be sold for $11 million, right? Not a chance. After foreclosing on the property, it may have been worth $4 to $5 million. Now it will come back in value, no doubt, but it may be a few years down the road and in the meantime the beast has to be fed.

Secondly, the building I purchased for my furniture store that was supposed to be the save-all if the store didn't work out has been a struggle. Why is that? It is a commercial building. Many of the businesses that could afford to rent it are no longer in business anymore and many of the business still around can't afford it. It is an $8,000 a month commitment and that takes a lot businesses out of play with that size of a monthly payment.

The same thing is happening in another commercial building I own. In it, there are five suites total with flex space of about 1,500 square feet to 3,500 square feet per suite. Great, those are smaller spaces for less money per month, but a lot of the smaller businesses are not around to lease the space anymore. I have spaces that I used to rent for $2,500 that I'm only getting $500 to $1,000 per month for now. Ouch!

All of this brings me to the point I want to make about what I've learned about real estate investing over the length of my career. After owning my three little white and green houses and having to deal with all the problems tenants in single family residences have, I was convinced that single family residences weren't worth it. I vowed never to own single family residences again because I thought of myself as too smart to be fooled twice into messing with those single family residence problems.

So instead, I found an acre and a half of land, built a 12,200 square foot building to put my lawn and landscape business on. I was sure commercial buildings were the only way to go. I started the furniture business, purchased a 16,000 square foot building, put $150,000 of tenant improvements into it and figured that the commercial building itself would be my Plan B if my furniture concept wasn't the second best thing since sliced bread. Then I went on to loan millions of dollars on vacant land and knew the worst case scenario would be to take it back and sell it for a profit. How tough could that be? I had it all figured out.

What I didn't take into consideration was what happens if no one wants the vacant land, if 20% of the businesses that can lease your space are gone overnight, if the space just doesn't fit what the businesses need, or if you almost can't even give it away as a rental. No one said to me, "Have you thought about these different scenarios," and "What is your fail-proof Plan B?"

So what does all this mean? What can we learn and more importantly, how do we avoid it and not have to live in fear every day that our investment may go bad?

The solution is actually very simple. It was the one thing that I thought I wanted to avoid the rest of my real estate investing career: **SINGLE FAMILY RESIDENCES.** I just wasn't investing in them the right way. I have that solution now that makes them almost hassle free, very lucrative and most importantly, the Plan B works *every time.* Really.

## CHAPTER 5

SINGLE FAMILY RESIDENCES – SOLVE ALL OR HORROR STORY?

et's review single family residences, which I will refer
to as SFRs, for a moment. Everyone needs a place to live. A
lot less people need a place for their business and certainly only
an extremely select few need non-income producing properties or
vacant land to develop. This means there is an abundance of people
looking for a single family residence.

Say we own an SFR and it rents for $1,500. Things start to slow
down in our neck of the woods and there are a few less people to
rent your SFR. Okay, maybe we can't get $1,500 anymore. Maybe
we can only get $1,400 or $1,300, but we're still getting $1,300.
We can find someone to rent the property in a matter of days, not
months and certainly not years. See the immediate difference
between SFR and commercial/non-income producing properties? This type of property is not in danger of going out of style or
becoming unable to be rented or sold.

One way or another, you will be able to get your property
rented. I can hear what you are saying about SFR in your head

right now, "Yeah, that is great, but I don't like messing with toilets, broken doors, water heaters that don't heat, dead lawns and all that fun stuff that being a landlord brings to the table with this type of investment." I hear you loud and clear; I don't like that stuff either. However, I have worked painstakingly for thousands of hours to develop and perfect a system that you can use to avoid most all of those nasty problems.

It is a Lease 2 Own program that eliminates all those hassles and switches the burden of those hassles to the Lease 2 Own Buyer. You want to know what the best part is? **The Lease 2 Own Buyer in our program is actually happy, even ecstatic, about having those hassles because they are treated just like the homeowner.** Think back to my first garage with all the lint covering every nook and cranny. It was messy, small and almost useless in ways, but it was mine, all mine! I loved that garage and still to this day have the fondest memories of owning it.

We are going to go way more in depth on how all this works later in the book, but for right now I wanted you to get a picture of what you can do by utilizing the information, secrets and tricks of the trade. As we lay out the whole foundation, you will learn to develop this type of real estate investment and build wealth for your family with very little risk.

With that very little risk comes very little in the ups and downs you normally would experience with the stock market or similar

INVESTING DOESN'T HAVE TO BE A ROLLER COASTER RIDE!

investment. The fear of opening your investment statements to see how you did this month is no longer there. Single family homes produce consistent, safe returns month after month and keep you off the rollercoaster of investing.

Remember, I told you that you could do this in any market and I would tell you how. That is the case and you essentially could get into any market and work this program. However, there are certain markets in which you shouldn't attempt this type of strategy. Don't get me wrong, it will work in any market, but I want to show you when and how to know that your down-side risk is still on the positive return side as we discussed before. No one complains (well they shouldn't) if their investment has dropped from 15% to 5%. I understand that is not ideal, but compared to the alternative of going into negative returns, it makes it a far superior investment. Let's get to the point that none of us have any fear of opening up our investment statements each month.

## CHAPTER 6

DON'T VIOLATE THIS ONE RULE

*H*ere is the key to knowing when you should be in the market and when you should be out. It is so basic and understandable I can't believe I didn't see this before when the market was so crazy.

The rule is only to invest when the market allows you to have sustainable rents for the value of the asset. That's it! Are you disappointed? Is it too simple? It is so simple I couldn't even fill a whole page for this chapter.

As long as you can reasonably get a positive cash flow for your investment (and you are almost guaranteed that because the type of asset/property you are going to purchase will always have a market for it), then, and only then, Plan B covers your downside.

As soon as you are buying properties hoping that you will make money because of appreciation or some big payoff down the road, then you are playing in a whole different ball game. Nothing wrong with that, but expect to go to bat sometimes in that game and find out the game has been changed on you and now you are playing football.

Know what you are getting into and what Plan B looks like before you invest. Like they say, "It's easy to buy things, not always so easy to sell."

CHAPTER 7

IT IS IMPOSSIBLE TO MAKE THOSE RETURNS

*H*ere is what I get told every day. It is impossible to make those kinds of returns with your program. I actually started telling people if that was the case, then you figure out what I did wrong, prove it to me, and I will buy a $100 gift card to your favorite restaurant for you. I have yet to part with $100.

I have to tell you, even my business partner, Steve Sixberry, wouldn't believe me at first. He is a super smart guy, pays great attention to detail, and owns lots of real estate himself. Prior to him becoming my business partner, it took months for me to prove to him that these returns were not only real but probably understated at times. I think a lot of times people like Steve, that are already savvy successful real estate Investors, have a harder time accepting that our Lease 2 Own system could outperform the conventional way of doing a regular rental or even a tradition-al lease option.

I am better today at explaining how all this works and why using a Lease 2 Own in the SFR market works so well with such little risk on the Investor's part and having very consistent returns. I think most people associate a higher return like 15% as being very risky and simply can't get past that notion. Yet, fabulously successful people know that there are times and ways to increase your return and actually lower your risk. This may seem counter-intuitive yet that is exactly what I have developed with my Lease 2 Own system. We are going to discuss how this works later in the book and how what I describe as "finding excess returns" in any investment can dramatically increase your return and actually lower your risk.

For some examples of properties that we have purchased using the Lease 2 Own Program, please see Appendix A at the back of the book. These show the property specifics and the actual rate of return.

CHAPTER 8

WHY NOT JUST CARRY A NOTE?

I am sometimes asked, *"Why not just carry a note or*
1st Trust Deed for the property and then you don't have any
of these hassles? True, you don't have any of the hassle or re-
sponsibility for the home, but you also lose control in a big way.
In this chapter we are going to get you way smarter than the
average bear.

First, you should never think about carrying a note unless the
purchaser/borrower is going to put down at least 30% or more.
Remember, you no longer have any control of the property. You
want your borrower to be heavily tied into the property and have
heavy penalties if they don't perform. Of course, one of the biggest
drawbacks for a borrower is to have to come up with 30% or more
as a down payment. There are people out there that are capable, but
it really limits your number of candidates.

What kind of interest rate will you charge for the note? 6%, 8%,
10% or maybe 12%. Wow, that is getting up there and most people
will not like the idea of paying really high interest rates.

"BESIDES BEING 'SMARTER THAN THE AVERAGE BEAR', WHAT OTHER QUALIFICATIONS DO YOU HAVE?"

So now compare that to a 15% plus return with a Lease 2 Own. Realistically, you are getting a better return with the Lease 2 Own than carrying a note, and the Buyer is much happier with the arrangement in a Lease 2 Own. The Buyer has been able to get into the home for much less than the 30% down required to carry a note. This is huge! It opens up the market with a much larger number of Buyers that have enough cash to get started in a Lease 2 Own, as compared to those Buyers that must come up with 30% down, in order to carry a note.

Most importantly, you are the one that is in control in a Lease 2 Own. If you carry a note and the borrower fails to pay the monthly payment, you are in for a long drawn out process of foreclosing on the home. That process will always be contingent on your state laws and political policy that are in vogue at the time.

Here in Nevada, it means it will cost between $1,500 to $5,500 for the foreclosure. You can serve them a Notice of Default after the number of days your Promissory Note states after non-payment on the Note. Then you must serve them a Notice of Default. The Notice of Default is 90 days long before you can take your next action. As of this writing, once they are served a Notice of Default they have the right to mediation in the state of Nevada. Mediation will drag the process out by two to six months depending on the wait period to get a date for a state appointed mediator to be available.

At the mediation, the borrower has the right to ask you to negotiate in good faith to resolve the issue. Whether anything comes of it, it will always drag out the foreclosure time.

Once the 90 days are up on the Notice of Default and the mediation has been completed, you will need to serve the Notice of Sale.

The Notice of Sale requires at least 21 days and public notices are posted. That is where most of your cost will be in making sure all the notices are served properly. You do not want to find yourself with some borrower that may have a propensity for suing you just to have something to sue you about. Following the law isn't easy and hiring a Trustee to do all the work is the only way to go if you find yourself in that position.

Finally, after all that is done, you need to decide how you want to set it up for the actual foreclosure on the courthouse steps and what price you will set as an opening bid. You will be able to bid up to the total amount owed to you plus penalties, late fees, accrued interest, etc. If that is high enough (meaning no one on the courthouse steps bids on the property), it will go through the foreclosure proceeding and you will receive the home back in your name with the title.

We are not done, and believe it or not, this is definitely the abbreviated version. You now have to get them out of the house. If they want to be stubborn about it, this may require hiring a lawyer to serve them and get them removed. They are considered squatters and you have to follow another whole set of laws to have them removed. How much fun does this sound so far?

Then, to add more salt to the wound, remember for the four months to possibly a few years during the foreclosure period on the property, they are not making any payments to you the whole time. I am irritated by just writing this scenario out for you.

It won't always be a nightmare. The process of foreclosing can actually go relatively smoothly and be completed in four months, yet it can also drag on if they fight you all the way and take up to a few years.

Now contrast that with a Lease 2 Own. If the Buyer stops paying the rent, it becomes normal eviction proceedings. Here in Nevada, it can be done in 14 days and costs somewhere between $40 to maybe a few hundred dollars. That's it!

Now you see why this becomes a no brainer from an Investor's point of view, yet it is a very fair and reasonable deal for the Buyer. I love those win-wins!

## CHAPTER 9

BEST TENANTS YOU WILL EVER HAVE

O ne of the extraordinary items about a Lease 2 Own done correctly is the quality of tenants you get to occupy the home, their home. That's the catch, it is their home in their mind and who will take better care of a home than the home-owner themselves?

Now, legally is it their home? Yes and no, depending on how you answer that. Yes, they do have an extended lease, usually 5 years, with a publically recorded interest in the home. That is the Memorandum, a very important part in the whole process, but we will cover the specifics later.

No, they don't legally own the home because our investment group or an individual Investor holds the title to that property. From a purely legal sense, we are the homeowner. However, as my business partner likes to point out, "What is the difference of them actually owning it by title and having a mortgage with the bank? Not much."

I know we are playing a little with the words and semantics

here, but the point is the Lease 2 Own Buyer feels, is treated as, and mentally is the homeowner. One of my best stories is from one of our Lease 2 Own Buyers that had gone through our program, found the house that fit them, and are now living in it.

They had really been through some tough times and were looking to be able to settle down and know that they weren't at the mercy of some landlord and a short term lease. They both had great jobs and long term employment, yet the husband had been fighting some type of cancer, so it had really been devastating on them both financially and mentally with everything they were dealing with health wise.

They found our program and thought this might be a way for them to get back on top, as they said. All of the sudden, what seemed to be such a bleak outlook was brightened with the prospect of owning their own home again and feeling safe and secure.

Here is the best part of what they told me. They were describing how it felt to be back into a home and some of the joys they were encountering. Then they said they had been out walking around the neighborhood meeting the neighbors etc. Without thinking twice, as they met the neighbors, they would point and say, "That is our new home over there."

Who do you think is the best tenant you will ever have?

The other aspect that makes a Lease 2 Own such a great investment property is that usually the tenants are investing their own time and money into improving and repairing the home.

Time after time, we are amazed at what the Buyers will do to their homes. They will completely transform it and really add a tremendous amount of value. This of course ties them in deeper and they are all that more committed to purchasing the home in the future.

We had one couple that had sunk $150,000 into their previous home. It was absolutely beautiful. They had a knack and the eye to make everything just right.

Unfortunately, they bought at the wrong time and were being forced to short sale their home. They joined our program and they found a smaller, much older home that needed a lot of work.

The place today is amazing. They basically said, "Get out of our way and we will transform this place back to beautiful," and they did. I asked the Investor that purchased that property in our program, "When was the last time in your other rentals you own that the tenant spent time, money and effort to fix up and beautify your rental home?" Of course, the answer from him was "Never."

There are times we agree at the time of purchasing the property that we will throw in money for them to use on an agreed upon improvement or repair. We monitor the progress and reimburse as we are given receipts for the work done. We are not going to just hand over a wad of cash and say, "Good luck." We are also always evaluating how savvy each of the Buyers are when they are telling us what improvements and repairs they want to do on their own. You just know which ones know what they are doing and which are hoping to know what they are doing.

In our contracts, they are responsible for all of the improvements: repairs and any kind of maintenance that surfaces after we have done the initial purchase of the property. This works two ways in most states because you have to remember you have only a tenant/landlord relationship at this point.

One is they take care of any of the repairs and maintenance needed. You never hear from them. However, in most states, they have the minimums you must provide as a landlord for your tenant, such as working hot water, working furnace, working toilets and sewer, etc. All the essentials that tenants would reasonably need to live in a home.

Now, again in our contract, they are responsible for all of those items, even if they are considered essential.

However, if they are not able to or willing to take care of one of those essential items, then by law within most of the states the landlord is required to provide them.

That is what happens, yet with a twist. An example would be the hot water heater going out and your Buyer calls to tell you. First, your response should be, "Sorry to hear that, but it is your home so take care of it." If the Buyer is not able to, then you need to fix or replace the broken hot water heater.

Whatever that hot water heater costs you to fix or replace is the amount that is added onto their purchase price.

Most of the time we find the Buyer doesn't want it to be added on to their price and will take care of the repair themselves, but not always. Sometimes they just can't afford it at the time.

We always purchase a home warranty plan when purchasing the home. These differ from state to state, but most of the times they will cover all of the major appliances from repairs to replacement with only a minor deductible of $40 to $75.

That keeps it affordable for the Buyer in case something goes wrong and gives them some peace of mind. The Buyers are also able to extend those warranties after the first year if they so choose.

## CHAPTER 10

"IF DONE CORRECTLY ..."

I *need to stress something here which is the importance* of when I say, "If done correctly, a Lease 2 Own can or will..." Those three words "If done correctly," are three very powerful words. I have talked to a lot of people over the few years that seem to think they know exactly what a lease option is and exactly how they work.

I know that is the case with a lot of those people I talked to but I also know that there are a lot of people who really don't know. Then there are a bunch that are even doing lease options, but are or have, really messed them up.

What makes me bring this subject up is the multitude of people I tell what I am doing and they start to tell me either their horror stories or more frequently what they have heard about lease option horror stories.

One of those stories is about when the Buyer doesn't end up purchasing the property and how they just go through destroying everything in the home. This seems to be about as prevalent as the

**911? WHAT DID I DO WRONG WITH MY
LEASE 2 OWN?**

myth of people pouring concrete down the drains when they are
forced into foreclosure.

I am sure it happens and I am sure it is not pretty when it
does, but I have yet to meet a person with a firsthand experience
of this. My point is, be careful about what you hear and what
you believe.

It is like the guy that dispenses all the advice to you about
some stock tip and hasn't made money trading stock in the last
10 years.

Let's get back to where we started and those three words, "If done correctly." You are going to see that continually throughout this book and that is because like anything else, experience is better than theory.

Here's another story from a friend in the business that thinks he knows lease options. What he really knows is he has found out a way to get more money out of his renter and that is all that matters.

First, he deals in the lower end housing. Not super low, but still that housing that you have to knock on their doors more often than not to collect the rent that was due 5 days ago.

He has bought a few of these places and has a good margin since they are on the lower end. Lower end always means higher margins, but also means more work.

What he has figured out is when he rents a place to someone, he suggests they pay $100 to $200 more per month in rent and he will set them up with a lease option. Then when they purchase from him, that extra amount paid will be credited towards their purchase, but remember, they don't get any back if they don't purchase. He writes up a simple little agreement to the deal and everyone is happy on day one. He is especially happy since he has been doing this for 25 years.

Do you know how many people have exercised their lease option with him? You probably guessed it, none. That's right, not one time has it happened.

You may or may not agree with his tactics. I can tell you I

don't. I think when you deal with people, you have an obligation to give them a fair shot at being successful. He is certainly not doing anything illegal, but you could say it is questionable.

This is also where a lot of the negative connotations come from with lease options. Now we are back to where we were talking about people destroying the homes before they left from an unsuccessful lease option. My guess is, that's happened to some extent because he has put those people in that position.

Notice that I use the words "lease options," when I am talking about the generic deals and usually in not so positive tones. That is specifically why I chose "Lease 2 Own" and not lease option for the name of our program.

We will talk further of how and why we do the things we do to qualify our Lease 2 Own Buyers, but that last story is one of the reasons.

I believe if you are going to run a successful long-term company, and in our case represent both sides of the table, I have to do it with the utmost integrity and each side has to have the best fighting chance to be successful. Otherwise it is all about squeezing the last dollar and not about building something I can be proud of for the long haul.

Maybe I feel that way because I was born and raised in the small town of Reno, NV? There you learn that you treat people right or it will come back to haunt you. My joke is, in Reno, if I sit down at the table and meet you and if we talk long enough, we will find out somehow that we are related. Okay, maybe that is an exaggeration but it seems true sometimes.

Those three words, "If done correctly," encompass a lot. Yes, it is the technical aspects of Lease 2 Owns, but they have to include the human aspects of how we work towards a win-win situation every time with all that are involved.

I do have Investors who have asked, "Why don't we just let everyone in the program because we would have a better chance of the Lease 2 Own Buyer not buying the house from us in the future? " In other words, we would have "Buyers that are failing."

That is just not the way I want to run the business. The Lease 2 Own Buyers in our program are terrific people with families, dreams, and the desire to control their own destiny which includes owning a home. I believe when you can get returns on your money that are really exceptional with so little risk, then take the deal and leave a little money on the table for the other guy.

## CHAPTER 11

HOW TO DETERMINE A BUYER'S PURCHASE PRICE

*T*here are many subtleties that you learn through setting up multiple Lease 2 Owns. Let's start to breakdown some of the technical aspects of how they are best set up. First, understand there are probably a thousand ways to literally set up Lease 2 Owns. Like always, this is a learning process in which you can't anticipate what all the outcomes will be until after the fact.

Let's start with basics of our program and then move into the variations. What I have always found is the simpler, the better. Yet for me, many times, it has to start complex first before it gets simplified. You fortunately get to have my refined simpler version and skip all the hard part of the trial and error. However, I find it to be an ever changing and evolving process with improvements to the system, so you are never fully finished!

Everything we are going to cover here is our most commonly used structure and can be reviewed and calculated with My Lease 2 Own Investor's Software. If you would like a free copy, email me at Greg@HughesCapital.com and include your name, full address, telephone, and email address, or send it to Hughes Private Capital 5440 Louie Lane #106 Reno, NV 89511. I will send to you the spreadsheet on a working CD. You will need Excel to run the spreadsheet. It is really quite amazing to be able to change the numbers to see how the returns change for you, the Investor.

Our Lease 2 Owns are usually held for 5 years. I figure that gives the Buyer enough time to turn around their financial situation and to get their credit repaired. It also allows the real estate market enough time to normally recover, appreciate, match and/or exceed the agreed upon purchase price for the Buyer.

Here is how we come up with the Buyer's purchase price. We take whatever, you the Investor, has spent to acquire the property in total and add 10% to that for the Buyer purchase price. That price is then locked in for 5 years for the Buyer.

What do I mean when I say "in total" for the Investor? You take the purchase price of the property you are going to pay, the closing costs, and any other costs like repairs or improvements you may agree to cover upon the purchase of the property.

Now, I would only cover repairs and improvements that increase the value of the property. Most of the time the Buyers will spend their own money on repairs and improvements, and of course, you want them to because it ties them more and more into the property.

Let's take a quick example:

Purchase Price for the Investor	$145,000
Closing Costs	$2,000
Flooring Allowance	$3,000
Total	$150,000
Add 10%	$15,000
Buyer Purchase Price	$165,000

Let me tell you how I came up with what appears to be a random 10% one-time increase to the Investor's all in purchase figure.

We tried this out many different ways and the 10% was the simplest and the most widely accepted by the Buyers. Initially we would do something like this: 6% in the 1st year and another 3% in year 3, 4% in year 4 and 5% in year 5.

You would have thought that the Buyer would like it better that way because if they could buy it in year one or two it would have never reached the full 10%. However, what I found was that they were always okay with what I added on for the first year. That just seemed to make sense to them and it was accepted. Adding later on really bothered the Buyer a lot more, as if just knowing it was going up in price really was a problem for them mentally in the future.

I know this sounds counter intuitive, but that is what I have experienced over and over. Of course, you can set yours up with whatever works best for you and what you can get your Buyer to agree to.

One of my objectives for the Buyer is to set them up into something that gives them as much "certainty" as possible. We live in an uncertain world and many Buyers are just getting out of a highly uncertain personal situation. The last thing they need is more uncertainty.

I think that one of the weird reasons is mentally they just know right up front it is 10% and that's it. There is no wondering what year they will be able to buy it and how much it will cost when that happens. I know logically that doesn't make sense, but we don't all think like Dr. Spock, especially when it comes to one of our largest life purchases: a home.

I have done many other variations to accommodate Buyer situations with what and when the mark up is applied to come up to their purchase price. Really, the only way to calculate these figures is to do this by running it through the My Lease 2 Own Investor's Software and finding out how that will affect your return.

This can be done in minutes. That is really how I have come up with all the variables, because each variable affects the return and so you need to work them all together depending on your situation to get the best return.

It is the secret sauce of knowing and understanding what your return will be when you change any part of the formula. I usually work it out or target so we have a 15% annualized return at the end of a 5 year lease, if the Buyer purchases the property. Prior to them purchasing the property, I target a 20% annualized return for each year. The reason it drops as each year goes by is because I have chosen the flat 10% increase on their purchase price and not any additional increases as we just discussed.

If the Buyer purchases in the first year or two, your annualized return is greater than if they wait until the fourth or fifth year. I don't like to see that fifth year fall below 15% most of the time.

One of the times you can adjust their increase percentage is when the Buyer is planning on purchasing it within or by the end of the first year.

That way you can usually lower the initial increase to about 4% to 6% and then do the additional percentages increase each year thereafter. I find it easiest to do 5% in the first year, then 5% in the second year and then hold that price for them for the next 5 years.

Warning: when making changes for people, don't set it up only thinking they will get their financing that first year. People are optimistic and if it doesn't happen you will have put them in a bad spot. Set it up like normal for 5 years and make sure to protect yourself if it continues into those additional years.

Another thing to be careful about is to make sure you are charging enough in rent if you lower their purchase price. We have not covered this yet, but our rent is 1% to 1.6% depending on the Buyer purchase price. Make sure you are charging enough rent if you lower their initial purchase price. I usually just figure the rent based on the full purchase price including the 10%.

## CHAPTER 12

RENT AND RENT EQUITY

L *et's look back to our example before of a Buyer's*
purchase price of $165,000. For this priced home, I normally
base the rent on 1% of Buyer's purchase price, so $1,650. That is
simple and easy to calculate in your head.

This is probably the number one item that a Buyer is con-
cerned about with their Lease 2 Own. It is the same for the Investor. If they can't make the monthly rent payments then everyone
has a problem. We are going to discuss later on how we determine whether the payments are appropriate for them and how we
qualify them.

You can see why properties that cost above the $200,000 mark
start to become expensive for the Buyer and actually for you too.
They start to eat up a lot of precious capital.

Out of the rent, we extend them Rent Equity of 20% every
month which is a credit towards their purchase. With our $1,650
example, the Buyer would be accumulating $330 in Rent Equity
every month.

This Rent Equity is not sent to the Buyer or stored in an escrow account. One of the mistakes Investors make is thinking the Rent Equity needs to be stored in an escrow account or some account that is earmarked for this purpose. It is actually the opposite of what you need to do and should do.

One of my friends who is a successful business owner who decided to go do a lease option, is storing his so called Rent Equity in an escrow account from advice from his brother who is an attorney.

Things can become muddy when it comes to doing this or not. I have been advised not to do it and here is why.

By putting the Rent Equity into some type of account and telling the Buyer about it, it could be construed as being their money. It's not theirs to use unless they purchase the property. Putting it into an account actually could give them the expectation that it is their money either way if they exercise their option or not.

You don't want to be fighting with them when they are moving out and they have decided somehow that it is their money that belongs to them.

Here is the kicker. There isn't any reason to ever store the Rent Equity in any account. The Rent Equity is not a cash item.

It only becomes a credit to them at the time of purchase, which will be, in technical terms, a debit on the HUD statement for you at the time of their purchase.

This is not cash you have to bring to the table. It is a seller's credit, a seller's concession, the seller is to pay the closing costs, etc. at the time the escrow is closed. I have found this to be a difficult item to understand even for friends that are successful business owners with an attorney brother. We went round and round on this one issue.

Since this is a non-cash item at the time of escrow, the title company will not be asking you to bring in any money (Rent Equity) to the closing. On the HUD it will show as a credit to the Buyer and a debit on your side of the transaction. I know this is getting a little technical and if you are not used to real estate closings and HUDs don't worry about it. Any good mortgage broker and escrow officer can explain how it works to you at the time of closing.

Now to make it more confusing, depending on the lender and the type of loan they are getting to purchase the home, they may or may not be able to use it for their down payment and closing costs.

The way that it is usually determined is by performing what is called a rent survey by an authorized real estate appraiser. These are usually not expensive. We pay around $75 for one.

The rent survey tells what the market is for regular rent in that type of home and area. What you want is the regular rent to be 20% or more below what you are charging them, assuming you are giving them 20% in Rent Equity. If it is more or less than 20%, I would adjust accordingly.

"IT WAS THEN THAT IGOR
DECIDED IT WAS TIME
TO STOP RENTING."

The lender wants to be able to justify that the additional rent being paid in the Lease 2 Own is greater than or equal to the amount of the Rent Equity.

The Lease 2 Own rent should be greater than the normal market rent they would be paying in a normal rental property by the amount of Rent Equities each month. If the rent they are paying is more than the market rent then the Rent Equity can usually be used towards their down payment and closing costs.

In my program, they never lose their Rent Equity whether

they can use it towards the down payment and closing costs or not. Sometimes, they can use them, but have accumulated so much in Rent Equity they will have some left over. Whatever that amount is in Rent Equity, it will be deducted off of their purchase price.

You can always make it work by reducing their purchase price, but most of the time the Buyers are going to be more successful when they don't have to come out of pocket to purchase the home.

I have found we have a much more difficult time getting our rent surveys to come in at least to the Rent Equity amount or more with our lower priced properties in the $75,000 to $115,000 range. We had one the other day where the rent survey was $1,150 and our Buyer's rent was only $1,067, plus they were receiving 20% in Rent Equity. Great deal for the My Lease 2 Own Buyer, but they will not be able to use any of their Rent Equity for their down payment or closing costs. We will reduce their purchase price by the amount of Rent Equity they have accumulated at the time of purchase.

Rent Equity is a beautiful thing. It works really well to help your Buyer to be more successful in purchasing the home, yet there is an unknown benefit to you, the Investor.

They are considered a non-taxable item until the Lease 2 Own is either exercised or not. The easiest way to think of them as a non-taxable item is they are treated similar to a security deposit.

A security deposit is not considered income until the lease has been terminated or any exchange has occurred with the security deposit and it has been recognized. Plus, at the time, when you do have to recognize it as income, it is considered at the capital gain rate.

*Understand I am not a CPA, and I don't even play one on TV. I am only relaying what we do at our company My Lease 2 Own, LLC and how we treat the Rent Equity portion. As always, consult your tax advisor to be sure it is right for you and that you are following the law.

The crazy part of having Rent Equity being a benefit for you is the higher they are, the more benefit they are to you as the Investor. That amount of the rent is not taxable, therefore the bigger the portion, the bigger the benefit to the Investor. If you can get your Rent Equity higher and give something else up, this can help to increase your return on your investment.

## CHAPTER 13

HOW TO TREAT AN ALLOWANCE FOR IMPROVEMENTS AT CLOSING

I *want to retrace a little ways back to our example* when I showed you how to calculate out the Buyer's purchase price. Remember the flooring allowance I used in the example? I want to make sure to make a point with you on how that is done.

You don't hand over $3,000 to your Lease 2 Own Buyer and say, "I hope it looks nice when it is done." Set it up so that you agree to provide the $3,000 when the flooring has been installed or they can produce receipts for the material and labor.

Only release that portion of the $3,000 that has been spent at the time. If you have any doubt, make sure to go physically inspect the property before releasing the funds. I know this sounds like common sense, but a lot of times this may not be what an Investor is thinking or know that it is another way to protect their return.

It is similar to the construction control voucher system. When a builder has taken out a loan to build a building, the lender will install a construction control system of some kind to monitor the progress of the construction and only release the money as the construction phases are completed.

Sometimes this is done directly through the lender and sometimes it's done through a third party. You can do it either way. If the project was extensive and you don't feel you have the expertise to judge how much of the construction was completed at different phases, then you may want to hire a third party that specializes in that to monitor the progress.

A word of warning: I have found throughout my career in real estate that you have to be very careful with third party construction control companies. They can be lazy and not even check the physical site. That, of course, is what you will be paying them for so make sure they are doing their job.

One of the ways they can prove to you they have physically inspected the job is through documenting every inspection and release of funds by picture of the project. Obviously, if the flooring portion is getting released, a picture of the flooring should be proof that it is actually completed.

Just like every business, there are good ones and there are bad ones. Get some references when possible but probably most of the time you should be able to handle it yourself.

## CHAPTER 14

IS A LEASE 2 OWN REALLY THAT MUCH BETTER THAN A REGULAR RENTAL?

*L*et me put it this way, "Friends don't let friends buy regular rentals."

I know one of the big things we have talked about is superior returns with a Lease 2 Own as compared to a regular rental. Like I said, a lot of times this takes some real convincing on the part of an Investor that has owned or still owns regular rentals. They are used to doing it the other way by buying regular rentals. When people are used to one way, sometimes it takes a little time to get them out of that box to look at a better, more profitable way.

One of those big reasons that makes a Lease 2 Own so superior is, you don't have 5% to 7% in closing costs. You avoid having to pay a sales commission when you sell to your Lease 2 Own Buyer. That is huge, considering what that does for your return on investment. The reason for no commission is the Buyer will purchase the home directly from you. There is no need for a real estate agent in the transaction the way we set it up.

STOP! DON'T BUY ANOTHER RENTAL

In fact, "if done correctly" then the Buyer should be able to get their financing and purchase the property without any outside source of assistance or the need for one. We set ours up so the old saying holds true: If we get hit by the bus, they don't need us to get the transaction done.

No commission-costs are a huge reason why Lease 2 Owns out-perform regular rentals, but let's review other reasons as well. Don't I need to convince you?

Treat your Buyer like they are the homeowner. You will get a great tenant, the best you have ever had and you will get them to be mentally prepared to act like a homeowner, as we have discussed before.

Here is the benefit of doing just that. When the Buyer is treated like a homeowner they will act like the homeowner most of the time. What kind of expenses do homeowners have that are different than regular tenants?

Sewer

Garbage

Home Owner Association Fees (HOA)

Property Taxes

Owner's Insurance

Maintenance

Improvements

That is one beautiful list of expenses that you, the Investor/landlord, would normally be responsible for and would directly eat into your return. In a Lease 2 Own, we have found that Buyers are willing, and almost expect, to pay for all of these expenses.

Just those alone will increase your return from any regular rental by 5% to as much as 10%. Yes, you are reading those numbers correctly. This is where I think a lot of real estate Investors that buy regular rentals say there is no way it can be that much.

If you still don't believe me on this, then send me an email at Greg@HughesCapital.com and ask for our report on Lease 2 Own vs. Regular Rental. Be sure to include your full address and telephone number. We will send you the report that shows you in black and white while actually color, why and how the Lease 2 Own out-preforms a regular rental every single time. It is impossible for them not to out-perform and have superior returns.

The other statement I sometimes hear from Investors is, "I want to own some regular rentals first and then I will do some Lease 2 Owns." What? Why would you want to do that? Remember, not everyone in the program will always be successful. For those that are not able to purchase the home from you, then there you go -- a regular rental. At least in the meantime, you collect above market rents, you have a superior return on your investment and now you can own the regular rental you wanted so badly with lower returns.

I have found most Investors do get it right away and understand they are choosing a superior investment with a Lease 2 Own over an inferior investment like regular rentals. I do think there are times that Investors just are not interested in which one is better, they just know a regular rental and they get lazy about improving their investment returns. I can guarantee that is not you or you wouldn't be reading this book.

Here are two more reasons as to why a Lease 2 Own beats regular rentals. One, is when you set up a Lease 2 Own it is formulaic. It is consistent and the return on your investment is known from day one. Because it is formulaic, you know that it works every time for every home. Using the same formula that ties all the variables together will produce the same result every time. From the second you put the offer in on the home, you know what your return will be as long as the Buyer stays and performs in the property.

On top of that, you have no speculation at all. You don't buy any home hoping that it rents out for X amount of dollars. You will have cash flow on your investment even before you purchase the property. The Buyer will be required to put money down prior to your purchase for the benefit of the purchase.

The second reason is that you don't have to do any of the work to find a property to purchase. Your Buyer will spend time and effort to find it themselves. After they have found their home, you do need to approve it and make sure what you will pay for the property is at least market value or less. The good thing about buying the property this way is the Buyer and Investor are aligned in their goals. They both want the best deal possible.

There is one last item that we go into greater detail later in the book that increases your returns on a Lease 2 Own as compared to a regular rental and that is, you don't pay taxes on the Rent Equity portion. As you collect that portion of the rent, it is non-taxable until either the option is exercised or not exercised. This alone will increase your return by 1.5% to 2.0%.

CHAPTER 15

CLOUDED TITLE NOW WHAT?

*L*et's discuss how the agreements and contracts
should be set up. There are two distinct sets of agreements
or contracts for every Lease 2 Own.   I tend to use the word
"agreements" because I believe it has a friendlier connotation for
both parties.

First, there is the regular lease agreement that you have with
any tenant. You have a landlord/tenant relationship and you have
a standard lease agreement. This is completely separate from the
Lease 2 Own agreements and all of its components.

The only aspect that is different from any regular lease agreement you would use normally, will be the timeline. Usually, these
will be much longer than a normal 1 or 2 year lease. As I have said,
we do most of ours for 5 years.

The second part is all of the Lease 2 Own agreements. There are
a few different agreements that comprise the entire package. Let's
review them.

LEASE 2 OWN HOMEOWNER'S AGREEMENT™

This is the meat and potatoes part of all the agreements. It is going to spell out all the terms and conditions on how the Buyer will perform and purchase the home in the future. I have outlined the main points of each of the documents for you below:

a) What type and how much consideration you are going to receive from the Buyer and how it will be applied.

b) Amount of Rent Equity and how it will be treated over the lease period and at the end of the lease period.

c) Who will pay for what and how? The how part is very important. We have our Buyers pay us additional rent within the rental lease agreement for the all the items below. The reason for this is if our Buyer were to be paying them directly to a vendor or government agency and decides to stop, then that will result in a lien on our property; plus, of course, there would be penalties and fines. This way we are always assured that they are getting paid and on time. Below is a list to work off of:

Sewer

Garbage

Homeowners Association Fees

Property Taxes

Owner's Insurance

Flood Insurance, if necessary

d) Whether you will allow them to pay down the amount owed and how you will treat that pay down.

e) Did you collect any extra money because the Buyer wanted to purchase a type of property outside the criteria you had set and how that additional payment will be treated?

f) How you calculate the Buyer's purchase price.

g) Does the agreement allow you, the Investor, to sell the property while the Lease 2 Own is in place?

h) Does it allow the Investor to encumber the property?

i) Is the Buyer able to assign or sell their portion of the agreement?

j) Where will the documents be held and how will they be executed?

k) Who will pay what costs at the time of the purchase between the Investor and Buyer? The names of the items below may be different in your state, but any good real estate agent or title officer will be a able to help draw up a complete list of closing costs as such below:

Escrow Fee

Transfer Tax Fee

Homeowner's Association Transfer Fee

Outstanding Liens

Assessments Current and Future

Owner's Title Insurance

Lender's Title Insurance

Appraisal

Inspection Fees

l) Buyer's purchase price schedule is attached at the end of the document. It is a spreadsheet showing the months of the lease with the amount of Rent Equity accumulated up to that point in time, if they were to exercise their option on that particular month.

m) All the rest of the fun legalese.

MEMORANDUM OF LEASE 2 OWN WITH OPTION TO PURCHASE

a) This document is the only one that is a publically recorded document. It states that the Buyer has an interest in the property. It is basically a lien on the property.

This is the most important document in order to protect the Buyer. Any Buyer should insist on having something publically recorded to protect their interest.

INSTRUCTIONS FOR TERMINATION OF LEASE 2 OWN AGREEMENT

a) States that if one of the reasons or situations below happens, then the title company is instructed to terminate the agreement and remove the memorandum from being a cloud on the title.

b) Buyer doesn't perform (i.e. pay their rent etc.)

c) You reach the end of the Lease 2 Own period.

d) Buyer vacates or abandons the property.

This termination document may be your most important document to protect your title. You will have a clouded title by having the memorandum recorded. If the Buyer vacates or abandons the property, you do not want to search the country trying to find the Buyer to sign off in order for you to remove the memorandum from the title. Same deal if the Buyer were to become hostile or non-cooperative because of a situation in their life. For instance, if they were to stop paying and refuse to allow the memorandum to be removed, the termination clauses would trigger dissolution of the agreement.

DEPOSIT AGREEMENT WITH MY LEASE 2 OWN, LLC

a) The full amount of their deposit and monies are due upon the acceptance of an offer for the home they have chosen to purchase.

b) If the Buyer decides to not move forward with the deal, they can request all their money back less any expenses and/or non-refundable amount prior to closing on the property. We have a $500, non-refundable portion if they choose to not complete purchasing a home.

c) If the Buyer decided not to move forward after the property has closed, then all of their deposit becomes non-re-fundable. Make sure they understand this and have signed off on it. I know it sounds silly that maybe a Buyer would go through all the work and hassle to have you buy the home and then immediately back out, but it could happen. We have not encountered it yet, but we did have a Buyer back out at 11:30 p.m. the night before. It ended up being a good deal that they did. They were going to be a problem from day one and we should have never allowed them to qualify. Lesson learned. The end result ended up being really great because since this was an approved short sale, we were able to delay the close by a few days. We then showed the home to some of our other Buyers that had been searching for a while but had not found a place. They took one look at it and said, "We will take it." We closed a few days later and had a better Buyer in it and happy Buyers that finally found a home.

d) It includes a mini HUD to specifically outline all the costs involved for the Lease 2 Own Buyer. We use this to spell out their amount owed and due prior to us purchasing the home they have chosen.

MY LEASE 2 OWN DISCLOSURES

Below are the questions covered in the disclosures:

a) What is a Lease 2 Own Agreement?

b) How is a Lease 2 Own Agreement different from an ordinary lease?

c) Does the Lease 2 Own Agreement protect the tenant against eviction?

d) Do I have to sign a Lease 2 Own Agreement if I only want to rent?

e) What are my landlord's obligations under a Lease 2 Own Agreement?

f) What are the tenant's obligations under a Lease 2 Own Agreement?

g) How can I find out if the homes' value is worth the purchase price in the Lease 2 Own Agreement?

h) What things should I look for in My Lease 2 Own Agreement?

i) Should I use a title company?

Make sure you have disclosures that clearly spell out the answers to those questions. If at any time a Buyer were to become disgruntled and possibly try to take legal action against you, you will at least be able to produce those disclosures for proof of some clarification. We have them initial after every item and we review them with the Buyer, one by one in our initial deposit meeting.

Lastly, make sure all of these Lease 2 Own documents are placed in an escrow account at a title company. That way there is no question as to where the documents are stored and when it comes time for the Buyer to purchase the home, it is a straight forward process; including if they don't purchase the property, then you have instructions to terminate as well.

## CHAPTER 16

HOW TO KNOW IF YOUR BUYERS ARE QUALIFIED?

W*e do this in a number of ways, yet it remains a* relatively simple qualification for the Buyers. It is nothing like they would have to go through if they were actually applying for a loan or a mortgage. Yes, they have to bring in certain documents (I will discuss later) so we can confirm their statements on income, their job and other pertinent information, but it is not as extensive as it would be if they were actually applying for a loan.

Our first step is that we initially want to learn all about their story and understand why they are in the position they are in today. We know everyone that is coming to us has an issue with credit. Some are horrible and have never paid a bill on time and others only have one glitch on their credit from a short sale with perfect credit all their life.

As much as we would like to have the latter, it isn't reasonable to only find that type of Buyer when you work with the volume we do. So how do we find great qualified Buyers in between the two mentioned above?

"YOU HAVE AN
INTERESTING CREDIT HISTORY.
I CAN'T WAIT FOR THE MOVIE."

First, if they are chronic late payers or non-payers they usually don't qualify. Why would the tiger change their stripes all of sudden? They don't. The pattern has been proven and we expect it to continue. They are not candidates for our program.

However, we find many people in between the chronic non-payers and the people that have just one problem from preventing them to get financing today. Here are a few examples.

We have many people that just can't seem to save up enough money to have a down payment, yet their income is sufficient to afford a home.

I had a lady that was exactly in that position. She never missed a payment and her and her husband made more than enough income to afford the home they wanted, but every time they had any money in the bank it somehow was spent on a new expensive toy, trailer, etc. You get the picture.

Now, they may still not be able to qualify for our program because they need some money for the Lease 2 Own fee we charge, but if they can, they stand a very good chance of being successful in purchasing their home from us because of the Rent Equity.

The Rent Equity acts as a forced savings plan for the Buyers and certainly increases their odds of being successful. So, for this lady and her husband they would probably be successful because they have what it takes to make the payments and don't miss them once they have the obligation. It is just that darn saving up the money and not touching the money trick they don't have down yet.

What are some of the other stories we hear? Some have had medical expenses that have wiped them out completely or almost. This is definitely one of the big ones we hear quite often. That is hopefully a one-time event once they have gotten past it and therefore they probably are good candidates.

Have they had a divorce? This is really common. Especially if the divorce was not the friendliest and they spent money on attorneys while splitting up their assets. We think that divorce attorneys might be a great place to market to find qualified Buyers, but we have not tried that avenue of marketing yet.

What other pieces of their story make sense or don't make sense as to why they would be successful in the purchase of their home in the future? You be amazed at what people will tell you, so don't be afraid to ask. In fact, usually they tell you way more than you want to know.

Once you know what their history and story is as to why they have a credit problem, it is time to understand about their income and job stability.

How much do they make?

How long have they been making that much?

How long have they been at their job?

What is the outlook for them to remain employed with
   stable pay?

This is mostly self-explanatory. If we have a person that has been at their job for 3 or more years and their income produces enough to meet our debt to income ratio, then that is the number one criteria as a predictor of whether or not they will be successful Buyers.

The reason their job, income, longevity, stability and their calculated debt to income ratio is the number one predictor of success, is that without that all lining up, they really don't have a chance. However, assuming all that does line up to the debt to income ratio, we want them repairing their credit score, which is not hard to do and is very mechanical.

If they use one of the credit repair companies that we work with, then they can expect to increase their score approximately by 10 points per month. (Be careful picking a credit repair company. There seem to be a lot of scams and not very good ones out there that people can waste their money with.) It is common for some of our Buyers only to need to get their credit score up by 30 or 40 points.

Remember, you may find Buyers that have their credit score at the level required to get a loan, but can't. If they have a foreclosure or short sale, at the time of this writing they can't get financing for three years no matter how good their credit is or how high their credit score. If they can get VA financing then it is only two years after a foreclosure or short sale.

If they have filed bankruptcy then it is two years. Yes, you read that right, if you have wiped out all your debt, you are rewarded with only two years instead of three.

Let's get back to where we qualify using a debt to income ratio. First, what does that mean? Anytime you see a ratio with whatever items preceding the word ratio, it means take the first item and divide it by the second item. Divide **debt** by **income** to get a percentage of their debt to their income.

We like to see a debt to income ratio (DTI) with their expected payments to be in the 43% range, including their housing costs of principle and interest payment, mortgage insurance premium (if any), owner's insurance, property taxes, and any homeowner association fees, plus all of their long-term debt based on their minimum monthly payment. Make sure when you are calculating the above figures that they are based on the monthly costs if you are using their monthly income.

If we have a Buyer with $75,000 in gross income we want their housing costs and long-term debt to be around $32,250 a year or a 43% debt to income ratio.

Let's breakdown an example of this debt to income ratio, but done on a monthly basis, since that is the way it is calculated:

MONTHLY

$6,250	Gross Income
$1,500	Principle and Interest or Current Rent
$144	Mortgage Insurance Premium
$40	Owner's Insurance
$125	Property Taxes
$45	Homeowners Association Fees
$210	Automobile 1 Payment
$340	Automobile 2 Payment
$283	Credit Cards (Minimum Monthly Payments)
$2,687	Total Considered Debt

$2,687 / $6,250 = 43% Debt to Income Ratio

The reason we use 43% as our debt to income ratio is that is the FHA's criteria as of this writing. We expect the majority of our Buyers to utilize the FHA loan opportunity when they buy their home, but let me be a little more specific. The 43% ratio is the preferred or ideal ratio that is used by a FHA mortgage broker. The FHA does allow the ratio as high as 49.9% depending on other factors such as their credit score, the amount of down payment, savings in the bank, etc.

Just like the FHA, we will have some flexibility on the 43% depending on the Buyer's net worth, such as if they have large amounts of savings, and/or they put a larger amount of option consideration monies down towards the purchase of the property. These factors help considerably depending on the situation.

We know that every one of these Buyers is coming to us because of a credit problem and we don't have to follow nearly as strict of guidelines as a mortgage broker would in order to get the Buyer financing through an FHA loan, but we don't want to qualify a Buyer that we know doesn't have any chance of being successful. That is not the way our program is set up and since most of these Buyers will use an FHA loan for their financing, we follow those guidelines relatively closely.

We calculate out three different debt to income ratios for our Buyers.

Current – Where are they now?

My Lease 2 Own Program – Where will they be once they are in the program?

Future – Where will they be after they purchase the home from us?

Here is what we derive from each of those places in time for their debt to income ratio. If their current one is low, which it is much of the time, then they should have some money saved up.

Many times this is due to them not having a mortgage payment for a period of time. If they don't have money saved up and they also haven't been making a mortgage payment, then that is a red flag. Sometimes that is due to them paying down debt and not saving the money. That may be a legitimate reason. Otherwise, if they haven't been paying down debt and they don't have any money saved up, then how are they going to pay the rent in the Lease 2 Own?

It is easy to control that their debt to income ratio doesn't exceed 50% at the time they enter our program. The way we control this is just the same way a mortgage broker does with a pre-approval letter when Buyers are getting a loan. We tell them what their maximum purchase price can be, therefore what they have been approved for in our program. Then we reduce that by 10% to arrive at the maximum purchase price we will pay as the Investors on a property. This works out very nicely since everyone knows where they stand as they go to find their home on the open market.

Then in the future when they are ready to get their financing and since it most likely will be an FHA loan, we keep their future payment for their maximum purchase price at an ideal 43% debt to income ratio. This shows us they have a real fighting chance of being successful in our program.

We calculate out the 43% debt to income ratio using a conservative interest rate. Because we don't know exactly when they will get their financing, we take the current interest rate today for a 30 year fixed rate mortgage and add 1.5% more to the interest rate. If the interest rates go up in the future, then we have somewhat prepared for it; if they don't, the Lease 2 Own Buyer will be that much better off.

One of the reasons they really should be successful is when looking at their debt to income ratio, in our Lease 2 Own program, <u>their current payment is going to be considerably higher than when they get their financing</u>. If they have been successful with us, then almost for sure they should be able to be successful with financing their home. This also motivates them to get their financing as quickly as possible making it a win-win for everyone again.

BELOW ARE THE BUYER'S REQUIRED QUALIFICATION DOCUMENTS THAT WE REQUIRE FROM ALL OF THE SIGNING MY LEASE 2 OWN BUYERS:

_____ Driver's license (or other I.D.) A photocopy of front and back will be made at application.

_____ Most recent 30-days' worth of pay-stubs from all jobs from all Buyers.

_____ Prior 2-years completed, personal tax forms with W-2's and all schedules attached.

_____ Prior 2-months asset statements (all pages) - checking, savings, 401(k), IRA, stocks, mutual funds, etc.

ADDITIONAL ITEMS:

If you own other real estate besides the property you wish to purchase:

_____ Copy of most recent payment coupon if property is mortgaged.

_____ Hazard insurance contact for each property owned.

_____ Copies of lease agreements for rental property that you own.

IF YOU ARE SELF EMPLOYED:

_____ Prior 2-years personal and business Federal tax returns

_____ Year-to-date Profit and Loss statement and Balance Sheet

_____ Copies of prior two years business license

IF YOU RECEIVE RETIREMENT INCOME:

_____ Copy of most recent award letters from each source of retirement income.

_____ Copy of check stub from most recent retirement check(s) or copy of bank statement showing automatic deposit.

IF YOU HAVE BEEN DIVORCED OR LEGALLY SEPARATED WITHIN THE PAST 7 YEARS:

_____ Complete signed copy of all divorce decrees and separation agreements, including any stipulations or modifications.

_____ If you receive child support or alimony: proof of receipt of child support for the past 12 months and that it will continue for at least 3 years (if you are using this income to qualify for the program).

IF YOU HAVE FILED AND/OR DECLARED BANKRUPTCY WITHIN THE PAST 7 YEARS:

_____ Provide a copy of petition decree, schedule of creditors, discharge and a letter explaining the reason for the filing or declaration of bankruptcy.

VA LOAN APPLICATIONS:

_____ Form DD-214 or, for in-service veterans, Statement of Service.

After we have collected all of the necessary documents, our staff fills out our **My Lease 2 Own Score** worksheet. From this worksheet we are able to produce the My Lease 2 Own Score for the Buyer which includes their debt to income ratio.

The My Lease 2 Own Score™ worksheet looks similar to this layout and there is a full layout of the worksheet in the appendix at the back of the book.

My Lease 2 Own Buyer:
Credit Report mid-FICO's:
Employer:
Job Description:
Current Gross Income:
Years Employed by Current Employer:
Date Verified Employment:
# of Type of Account on Joint/Individual Credit Report:
# of Positive Accounts:
# of Derogatory Accounts:
# of Public Records:
# of Credit Reports ordered in prior 12 months:

Investor's Purchase Price plus Closing Costs:
Maximum Approved ML2O Buyer's Purchase Price:
Debt-To-Income Ratios:
Current Rent or Estimated Principle and Interest:
Mortgage Insurance Premium:
Property Taxes:
Owner's Insurance:
Home Owners Association Fees:
Long-Term Debt (Monthly Minimum Payments):
Total Considered Debt:
Source of and Proof of Funds:
Estimated # of Months for Buyers to get Financing:
Notes and Special Areas of Concern:
My Lease 2 Own Notes:
Review by Mortgage Advisor:

Once all of that is complete, we will have a mortgage broker pull their credit report and work through their file just like he would if he were to give them a mortgage. Yet, like I said before, it is a much easier process.

We complete the My Lease 2 Own Score by having a mortgage

broker be a third party to the transaction. They review the file, the credit report and then record their final opinions. From the My Lease 2 Own Score, we are able to decide whether or not the Buyer fits our criteria and their level or chances of success.

*NOTE as to why the mortgage broker has opinions: you would think that this is a mathematical problem and nothing more. He is to review the documents, calculate out a debt to income ratio, figure out when they can get financing, etc. There is always the human part and every time the mortgage broker is required to speak with the Buyer(s) and listen to their story, just like we have, he listens from a mortgage broker's perspective. It sometimes will have a completely different twist than what *we heard or saw* as we listened to their story.

Let me give you a really good example of this. We had a potential Buyer that was getting close to retirement and was hoping to own his first home. He had worked for a public bus system for the last 20 years and was going to have a nice pension to retire on.

His retirement income was going to be sufficient for the type and size of home he was interested in. Everything looked like a go as we traveled with him through his story.

After the mortgage broker spent time on his file and listened to the story from his side, a few things started to emerge. First, he was trying to improve his credit. That's good, but he really didn't understand what he was doing. He had started to open up credit card accounts all over town and was starting to carry a balance on them. Strike number one as to why he thought this was a good idea. It showed a complete lack of financial understanding.

Secondly, his credit report started to show a few aliases. We always use the tri-merged credit report that only a mortgage broker is able to access. It provides much more detailed information that is needed when we are qualifying our Buyers. With this Buyer, we were starting to find aliases that didn't make sense. That can be a red flag and sometimes it can just be an anomaly on the report. This guy had too many of them and couldn't explain them.

Needless to say we didn't qualify him for the program. We would have never found those items unless the mortgage broker had pulled the tri-merged credit report because they won't show up on a regular credit report. The mortgage broker's perspective is invaluable. Get help with this part of the process and get an expert's opinion to be reviewed along with the information you've found.

Lastly, not only are we able to decide on their qualifications from the My Lease 2 Own Score, but it also tells us some other really important items. It tells us when they will be eligible for financing in the future, assuming they work on their credit scores and bring them back to the minimum number they need for a loan. It also tells us by using a conservative interest rate, usually about

1.5% more than the current rate, of how much they will qualify for in the price of a home.

Once we have put together all this information, we can steer them into the right sized home and they can start to plan and work on getting their credit repaired for the day they will be able to get their financing again.

I know this chapter has been long and filled with a lot of information, but I can't stress enough how important this step is in the process of putting together profitable deals and hopefully avoiding headaches down the road.

.

## CHAPTER 17

MARKETING TO LEASE 2 OWN BUYERS

*T*here are multiple ways to waste your money and there are multiple ways to use your money wisely. I will review what has worked for us and what has not worked so you can make your decision for what may be best for you.

How many Lease 2 Owns do you want to do? Obviously, if you only want to do one then this shouldn't take all that much effort. There are many people and families that want to own, but can't, no matter what the economy is doing. People will always have some type of situation that results in a credit problem.

Our best method of finding Buyers has been working with real estate agents that are the go-getters in our community. This is really another one of those win-wins, because if a real estate agent comes across a Buyer that can't get financing, then they really can't do much with them. They might be able to find them a home on the market that the owner is willing to do a lease option on, but those are few and far between. Think about what the chances are, that the one owner that is willing to do a lease option fits the Lease 2 Own Buyer's wants and desires in a home. They are slim.

However, if you were to open up the option for the Lease 2 Own Buyer and the real estate agent to go find a home anywhere on the open market with some criteria you set, then their world just changed for the better. In this case, you will want to have the real estate agent do all the normal real estate agent stuff and collect the commission on the Buyer's side. What I would definitely recommend is: Do not let the real estate agent draw up the Lease 2 Own Agreement, even if they tell you they have done it before.

We find that most real estate agents think they know how to draw up a lease option because they will use a standard form that is provided to them or one they have bought as a standard form. You are asking for trouble with this type of agreement. Follow what I have outlined for you in this book and it would be best to find an attorney to draw up the agreements for you.

Now I know with that last paragraph, the hair on the back of your head just stood straight up and you probably got a sick feeling. I know, I don't like to have to pay attorneys any money, ever, but sometimes it is the smartest thing to do. You should be able to find an attorney that can draw it up for less than $1,000 and advise you on what to do. It will be worth it, but yes, painful. (Sorry to all the attorneys out there reading this book. Don't take it personally.)

The reason that real estate agents are such a great source for finding Buyers is obvious, I think, but let me point out something that may not be completely obvious. It is the relationship and trust that the Buyer has with that real estate agent that is your real ace in the hole. The Buyers don't know you and they all start out very skeptical because usually the program sounds too good to be true to them. That relationship with the real estate agent really helps to move them along in the process.

How do you get started with real estate agents? The old fashioned way: start calling the ones you know and talking to them about what you want to do. **Forewarning: you are going to have to explain the program to them.** *They are not going to understand it, and if they do, they will think it is just a simple lease option and you know that couldn't be further from the truth.* I spoke about this earlier in the book about how all these people I talk to say, "Oh, sure a lease option. I know how those work." They might know how they work, but not the way we structure them.

The other thing that real estate agents are going to try to talk you into is just buying a home and renting it out. Yes, a regular rental. They will do that because, again, that is what they know. They look homes up on their database, put you in the car, show a few of them and expect you to just buy one hoping you'll rent it out. That is what they know and that is the easiest way for them to get paid their commission. This doesn't make them bad people; it just makes them frustrating to deal with.

"YOU'RE A GOOD REALTOR AND TRY HARD, BUT SOME OF YOUR IDEAS ARE A LITTLE BEHIND THE TIMES."

After you find a few and get them trained to the way you want them to put together a deal, they may be your best source for deals. Be patient. It may take longer than you think to get this established and get them trained for how to find the Buyers and bring them to you.

One last comment on real estate agents: be prepared to have to talk to quite a few of them before you really get one to start working with you. When I started my program, I recruited 65, what we called, "Certified Lease 2 Own Real Estate Agents" into our program. They were required to pay us a fee to become certified and a portion of their commission when they found a Buyer for the property. Just like always, only a few of those recruited ever did anything. The number is very low. Only about 10 out of the 65 are active and then it is really only 5 out of those 10 that make deals happen.

It always comes down to the 80/15/5 Rule. You have heard of the 80/20 rule where 20% will make 80% of the money in almost any given endeavor. The 20% breaks down even further to 5% earning the majority of the 80%. It works out this way every time. Like I said, be patient and you will find some really good real estate agents to work with.

There is a funny story with our certified real estate agent program. When we started the program, we knew if real estate agents were going to help us to be an important part of our marketing strategy, we needed to get them trained to the specifics of our program. We started marketing to the real estate agents, telling them if they joined our program, *which was done through our own certification,* they would be certified to market to Buyers and collect commissions.

We, of course, made up this certification to what we wanted and nothing more, but many real estate agents are conditioned to believe they need all these fancy letters after their name to sell more real estate. Yet, the only people that care about those letters after their name are the real estate agents that received them and the outfit that charged the real estate agent for them. Joe and Mary, the home Buyers, couldn't care less. They just want the home they picked out for their family. That was fine with us because it worked to our advantage.

We were completing one of our trainings, in which the real estate agent will be "officially certified" by us and will have their grand new title of "Certified Lease 2 Own Real Estate Agent." This enables them to participate in our program and market to Lease 2 Own Buyers. A real estate agent raised her hand and asked, "Is this a *state* or *federal* certification?" I kid you not. I told her with as much of a straight face as possible that it was a "universal certification" and it is the only one you can receive in real estate.

Other marketing can include taking it directly to the Lease 2 Own Buyers themselves. The best way is to find a targeted list that will have the most people that could be Lease 2 Own Buyers. That could include renters, people that have just been through or are still going through a short sale, people that have lost their home to a foreclosure, people that have had a bankruptcy, divorce attorneys, mortgage brokers, Craigslist, landing pages built to collect information from Buyers, a website, etc.

Finding the best targeted list is very important. The more targeted the better. Everyone is dealing with the same challenge in any kind of marketing. You need to spend less on your marketing than what you make in the revenue you produce. For every dollar you spend on marketing, you should be able to produce ten dollars or more of revenue. That is a good ROI on your marketing. It won't always happen, but it is a goal to shoot for.

Also, nothing should ever be done without measuring the results. Don't fall for any kind of advertising ploys from anyone talking to you about it building up the brand or awareness. It either produces direct results for you or not. Unless you have millions to blow (if you do, please contact me) then you need to make every dollar count and the only way to do that is to measure your direct results.

This is why the target list is so important. Let's use an example. You want to send out a nice postcard to some renters to let them know about your program. So you call a friendly list broker and pay $600 for a list of 3,000 renters in your area. Now, you are all fired up and ready to send your postcards. So you have it designed, printed, labeled, delivered to the post office and you sit back waiting for the phone calls to come rolling in. No one calls except one guy that didn't understand the program and thought he could do it for normal rent and still buy the house. So now what?

Well, that was expensive. $600 on the list, $200 to design, $1,000 for printing and labeling another $150 for the delivery to the post office, and $750 on postage: $2,700 and nothing to show for it. Figuring a 10 to 1 ratio, you should have produced at least one to two Lease 2 Own Buyers. This may be a little extreme, but not an unreasonable outcome to expect.

Marketing is not a one-time event; it has to be repeated over and over. *As you repeat it over and over,* your material and your marketing becomes *recognized* and *familiar.* **Now a phenomenon starts to take place and it is truly no less than that. The more they see your marketing, the more familiar they become with you. The more familiar they become with you the more they begin to trust you. The more they trust you, the more reasons to finally take action to contact you and find out about the program.**

Familiarity breeds trust. I have on my Outlook calendar every Monday morning a reminder that says, "81% of sales are made on or after the 5th contact. 90% of sales people never make the 5th contact." The key is building that trust with your market, so therefore you must be able to send, deliver, or make contact with your market multiple times.

This has proven that a multiple step marketing campaign is more successful than one sent out one time hoping for the best. We don't have enough time to teach you all the marketing techniques in this book, far from it. There have been probably tens of thousands of books written on it, but I am going to take the time to review the basics so you can then go do some more research on your own.

I would suggest starting with one of Dan Kennedy's books on sales or marketing. He is hands down the best marketer I have ever seen, and I do a tremendous amount of study on this subject. You might start with his book on *No B.S. Direct Marketing* and then subscribe to his newsletter to get doses of his marketing genius every month. Don't stop there with Dan Kennedy. Get his other books. I have never found one of them to be anything but a <u>great value</u>, that you should read over and over again. I would also suggest reading *The Ultimate Sales Machine* by Chet Holmes. Holmes is a master marketer as well and his book will fill you with hundreds of ideas.

One of Kennedy's basic teachings on direct marketing is the multi-step campaign. This means sending something to them multiple times with some type of follow up copy, which builds on the previous ones. You send the postcard first, then a long sales letter, and finally follow it up by another postcard or letter. What you will find is the response rate goes up each time the marketing material is sent.

Say on the first postcard you receive a 1% response: a typical, if not good response. However, when you send out your second mailing, maybe as a long sales letter (by the way, long copy out performs short copy almost always), you might find that your response rate will climb to 2.5%. Not just on your second mailing, but on the first and second one combined. Then with the third mailing, the same thing gets your response rate up ever further.

This gets to the reason why the targeted list is the most impactful for your marketing success. The more targeted, the more responses, right? Of course, but the more targeted also usually means a smaller number of prospects on that list. The smaller the number of prospects to send a direct mail piece to, the more pieces you can afford to send. Plus, you'll be able to spend more per prospect to attract them to your program.

One of the best ways to get started with a list you have decided to use (a whole book could be just written on the targeted list) is to start with a small amount of names from it.

We could go back to, as an example, the list we purchased of 3,000 renters and randomly only choose 100 to 500 names from that list to start with and send the marketing campaign to them. Evaluate your response and tweak your campaign as you go along. This allows you to spend less money and test your marketing materials.

Word of caution: when sending out a small test batch, it is possible, if the sample you chose is too small, that you may not receive much response even though your marketing campaign may be just fine. It is a numbers game. If you sent out only 100 and didn't receive any kind of response compared to sending out 1,000 to the same group with the same marketing material and receiving 10 responses, you received a 1% response rate with 1,000. Obviously, the 100 could have just not had one of the ten responses in it.

So don't throw it all away, right away, if at first you don't get the response you want. This is why marketing is not black and white and you have to keep tweaking. When you do tweak it, it is best to only change one thing and test it again. If you change more than one thing at a time, then how do you know which one worked? You don't. Work this like a science experiment and track everything as best you can until get that right formula.

Let's go through some of the other marketing methods and sources. Lists of homeowners who have been through a short sale or foreclosure are available. Places to obtain the lists would be list brokers, title companies and credit companies like Equifax. Another way to put together short sale lists is to have your real estate agent print off all the active short sales in the real estate database and send them direct mail to market to them.

For a list of renters that you probably won't have to pay for, go to the title company and ask them to print you a list of non-owner occupied homes. You can give the title company just about any criteria to further break that list down.

People who have gone through bankruptcies are going to be a lot sketchier as to their quality, but there again, listening to their story is important. Remember, it can be as simple as a medical issue that forced them to declare bankruptcy and now it is all behind them. Plus, after a bankruptcy, they usually don't have any debt left, so their debt to income ratio is excellent. You could market to bankruptcy attorneys and let them know about your program. You definitely will be able to get lists.

You can do the same with divorce attorneys. Divorces are a big reason why people's credit gets messed up, or maybe it is the other way around. Maybe because they have such messed up credit, it caused the divorce? I don't know, but either way that may be another marketing avenue to pursue.

We have used Craigslist ads. You can advertise other homes that are for sale and put an ad in for the Lease 2 Own to drive calls for your program. It is actually an ad of an actual home for sale. This is legitimate, since if you find a Lease 2 Own Buyer and they are qualified, they might want you to buy the home for them as the Investor. Secondly, with Craigslist ads you can add additional teasers on the ad such as an "Available Lease 2 Own Homes" link. Build a landing page, so when they click the link it will explain to them how they can find a home on the open market. Your landing page should offer something else, like a free report, so you can capture their email address.

Developing a website may be useful. I would be careful here about spending too much time on one unless you are really going to do a lot of volume. The number one reason for a website is to gain credibility. Yes, it is there to give them information, yet most people go to the internet to learn more about you and your company to understand if this is a scam or if it's legitimate.

Most Lease 2 Own Buyers are skeptical from the beginning. It usually sounds too good to be true and they most likely don't know you at all. You have to get them to the "Okay, this is not a scam" stage before they can start listening and understand the program. Just don't spend a lot of time or money on a website. It will not be what will drive any business through the door for you. It will be there mainly to just legitimize you.

Mortgage brokers could be another source for leads. The broker(s) you work with to qualify your Buyers for sure should be. Then a marketing campaign to others will most likely prove successful over time. They are a little like real estate agents, very focused on the one way they can do deals and have a hard time getting what you are doing.

Figure out if in your state, you can compensate them for sending you a referral. Usually you can, because the Lease 2 Own program doesn't have anything to do with a loan. Plus, if the mortgage broker is smart and forward looking, they will understand they should be getting to do the loan for the Buyer when they can get financing in a few years.

One other benefit for mortgage brokers is sometimes you may send one of your Buyers down to them to get qualified for the program and they find out they can get the potential Lease 2 Own Buyer financing today. That's great for everyone. They get a loan and the Buyers get to go buy a home.

There are a few methods that are not as targeted, but yet cost effective. The post office has a program called "Every Door Direct Mail®" that will target certain carrier routes. You don't have to own a bulk mailing permit and can mail up to 5,000 flat mailers per day. As of this writing, the cost is only 14.5 cents per piece delivered by the USPS and they can be oversized. Your marketing piece will be delivered in whole to the carrier routes you designate without any address labels or names. There are companies out there that will put this whole campaign together for you right up to delivering them to the post office bundled and ready to go.

This can be an effective way to market even though it is not targeted like we have spoken about previously. You can target certain neighborhoods that may have the most potential Buyers. Those neighborhoods would usually be the ones built during the boom and now have the largest amount of people that are underwater in their mortgage.

There is a definitely an added benefit with this type of marketing and that benefit is almost all these people know someone else. If they are not a candidate for the program, then they can pass on the information. Because of this, make sure your marketing includes something saying, "Do you know someone that has been through a short sale, foreclosure, bankruptcy or is tired of renting?" You want to put the thought into their mind.

Another method that we have found effective is targeting neighborhoods with door hangers. We have found it costs us about the same to have door hangers delivered as it does the Every Door Direct Mail®.

Remember, the same marketing rules apply for this type of delivery – you have to hit them multiple times. You will get some good responses from the first delivery, but keep delivering them to boost your response. With door hangers, we design our own and then send them off to an online printing company. If you are good at getting the design done yourself or have someone that can do it for you, using an online printing company is an easy way to get your marketing materials produced.

That should give you a great head start in your marketing, yet there is so much more to know. I really encourage you to become a student of marketing and constantly be striving to improve on it. It is definitely more of an art than science to really get it right, yet the science is how you will measure the art side. I can't stress enough that you need to know your metrics and your ROI for each of your marketing campaigns.

CHAPTER 18

HOME WARRANTY AND
CREDIT REPAIR

*W*e always purchase a home warranty for the first year for our Buyers when we purchase the home. It certainly seems to be a peace of mind for them and many of the Buyers say they will extend it for the following years on their own.

Usually, the warranties will cover major appliances such as the furnace, dishwasher, air conditioner, garbage disposal, hot water heater and other necessary repairs. They charge a deductible of $50 to $100 per repair or replacement and the Buyer is responsible to pay for the deductible.

All sounds like a great deal, right? That is until you need to get something fixed or replaced. We have found that the home warranty companies lack sufficient enough coverage.

Let me give you a real life example. We had a hot water heater stop working and it was determined that it would need to be replaced completely and not repaired. Great, our Buyer was to pay their deductible, happily have a new hot water heater installed, and have it paid for from the home warranty we purchased. Not so fast.

The plumber that was to do the replacement wanted $949. The home warranty company informed us that they would only cover $589 for the replacement less the $70 deductible, netting out only $519 they would pay for the hot water heater. That was leaving our Buyer with $430 of an out pocket expense.

Needless to say, our Buyers weren't happy. In discussions with the plumber, this happens all the time. We have dealt with the same issue multiple times over the years where the repair or replacement far exceeds the amount the home warranty company is willing to cover.

Here is a suggestion on how to solve this dilemma, but before we do, let's skip to our credit repair subject. I will come back to how you can solve the home warranty issues.

Of course, all of your Buyers will need to repair their credit from as much as 150 points to maybe as little as only a few points. As mentioned before, there are credit repair companies out there that are very effective in doing this for consumers.

Probably the best way to find a good credit repair company is to ask the mortgage brokers you know. They may be working with one or two and should know how well they perform for their clients. A good credit repair company, with the cooperation of Buyers, should be able to increase the Buyer's credit scores by 5 to 20 points per month.

This usually means they don't have to work with them for a long time before their credit scores are where they need to be in order to get their financing. The credit repair companies usually charge an initial set up fee and then a monthly fee. The monthly fee is during the period of time the Buyers need to get their credit scores to at least the minimum required number for their financing. This obviously can be a great benefit for your Buyer.

So why am I combining the home warranty and credit repair into the same chapter? Here is a way for you to solve both of the challenges of poor home warranty coverage and needed credit repair together into one program for your Buyers.

Require, or make optional, which ever you prefer, your Buyers to pay you a monthly fee to cover the home warranty and the credit repair program. Give it a name like, "Your Peace of Mind Program".

It doesn't matter what you call it, or if you name it at all, but you want it to represent value for your Buyer. You will probably want to charge $59 to $99 per month and I would do it for the entire lease period. It just becomes another monthly payment like sewer, trash, owners insurance that they are used to paying and protects them from repairs and assists them in getting their credit repaired. Maybe you can even find some other services or benefits to add, to create as much value as possible for your Buyers.

Here is how the math works for such a program. We pay usually $350 to $500 for home warranties and they come with $50 to $100 deductibles. Understand these companies don't do this because they are kind or non-profit. They are profitable at those prices, but don't cover all the costs.

If you charge $79 per month, that is $948 per year; almost double what the normal home warranty costs. You will need to do some research in your area if you don't know these figures off the top of your head. Then when something does go wrong, you should be able to cover more of the repair expense or replacement value. I would still charge them a deductible because it is always best when people have to pay at least some of the costs.

As for the credit repair, find a good company and offer the service to them as part of this program. Most likely you will only have to pay for it 3 to 9 months and their credit should be back up and ready to get financing when the time comes.

This really can be a win-win for everyone. You can make a little more money on your investment and your Buyers will feel more comfortable knowing they are covered for major repairs, all while being assisted in getting their credit repaired to buy their home.

## CHAPTER 19

IS IT LEGAL WHERE YOU LIVE?

*L*ease 2 Owns are identified by many different names. Some names are correct and some are not as a true Lease 2 Own. The most common name is usually a "Lease Option." Then there are Rent to Own, Land Contracts, Owner Financing, Installment Sales, Executory Contracts, etc.

Owner financing is probably the most mixed up name that is not a lease option, but is construed as one by the general public. Of course, the difference being that owner financing is an actual loan for the Buyer and the Buyer holds title.

Be sure to check with your local regulatory agencies to follow any laws you may have in your state. As an example, Texas has relatively new laws making it harder to do Lease 2 Owns, but not impossible. They are referred to as an Executory Contract, which changes many of the implications for Buyers and Investors. These make it easier for a Buyer to hire a lawyer and win against small mistakes made by the Investor.

Your state may regulate other items. For example, sometimes

a lease option can be considered a sale upon the signing of the option and the Buyer receives all the tax benefits while the Investors have to own the property as Fee Simple. Another is if you encumber the title, you have to tell the Buyer everything, including how much you pay per month, and the Buyer has to approve it.

Illinois and North Carolina have such strict laws, they say this makes a lease option "functionally illegal." In Colorado it is illegal for the seller to write the land contract, instead an attorney must write it.

You can do a lease option in every state, but some states will be riskier and harder than others, with fewer benefits and more restrictions. The bottom line is to find out about your state laws so you are protected. A good place to start is with a good real estate attorney or your governing body for real estate regulations.

## CHAPTER 20

FINAL THOUGHTS

Completing *Lease 2 Owns can not only be a very* lucrative financial move on your part, but it has the added benefit of helping people and their families achieve their homeownership dreams. So many times, it is easy to get caught up in putting the deal together, running the numbers, inspecting the property, checking credit scores and all the other technical aspects that you can forget there are people on the other side of the equation. Remember that you are going to provide an opportunity that maybe they can't find anywhere else.

I know this happens for me. I am so busy running the businesses and making the deals that after we get a family into a home and we ask them for a testimonial, it blows me away every time. They talk about how it has opened doors that weren't there before having their own home. They talk about how it gives them the feeling of security and stability. They show off what kind of improvements they have done to their home. They are proud of what they have accomplished as well.

Literally, it has brought a tear to my eye and goose bumps all over my body when I stop and really listen to the good that is provided for people and their families with our Lease 2 Own program.

A home is the American Dream and to feel hopeless that it will never come true for a person can be a devastating blow to their confidence, ego, ambition and truly their success in life. I know this doesn't apply to everyone, but for those that connect with the homeownership dream, it is a powerful moving force in their lives.

From me to you, helping people and their families to live their dream is extremely satisfying and fulfilling, along with the added benefits of it being a profitable way to invest your money and to spend your day.

All the best,

Greg Hyde

APPENDIX

TO CONTACT GREG HUGHES:

Hughes Private Capital, LLC

My Lease 2 Own, LLC

5440 Louie Lane Suite 106

Reno, NV 89511

(775) 297-4977

Greg@HughesCapital.com

www.HughesCapital.com

www.MyLease2Own.com

INVESTMENT – any vehicle or item you must put money into expecting to get a positive return of your principle and including additional monies over and beyond your principle usually known as your return.

PRINCIPLE – the initial and additional amounts of money or capital invested into the investment. Sometimes defined as a your capital investment.

PROFIT – the amount of money that is greater than your principle in an investment at any time.

LOSS – the amount of money less than your principle in an investment at any time.

CASH FLOW – monies generated from an investment that actually represent useable cash. Not a paper return or profit that is only actualized if the asset is sold. It is actual cash generated from the investment without the sale of the asset.

PLAN B – your back up plan for any type of investment. What will you do in the event that the investment doesn't go as planned? Possibly one of the most overlooked yet important parts of being a successful Investor is to never enter an investment without Plan B. Plan B will expose your downside risk for evaluation.

UPSIDE – the potential profit an investment can produce. Most investments that have almost no upside potential have very little risk associated with them. Usually, the greater the upside the greater the risk, but not always.

SPREAD – the difference between the actual or anticipated return for an investment and the risk. The further you can, as an Investor, increase the spread the better the investment. Investors have become wealthy by exploiting this one aspect.

RETURN – the amount or lack of profit received on an investment expressed commonly in a percentage. $100 investment with a return of 10% would represent a $10 profit.

ANNUALIZED RETURN – the return expressed in a 12 month figure. If your return was cumulative 10% for the last two years then your annualized return would be 5% per year.

INTERNAL RATE OF RETURN (IRR) – a more sophisticated return, taking into consideration the timing of the cash flow received throughout the period of the investment including the sale of the asset. Generally, the sale of the asset is projected in order to produce a forecasted IRR.

HAPPY INVESTORS – those that meet or exceed their goals

when investing. They have received what was expected or outperformed the initial forecasted results.

ANGRY INVESTORS – those that have failed to reach their goals when investing. Can be angry with themselves or with others that have enticed them into investments that were poor with no spread. They usually only understand it after the fact of investing. The worst of all being in a high-risk investment with low upside potential.

RESIDENTIAL PROPERTY – any properties used to live in. Could include single-family residences (SFR), condominiums, duplexes, apartment buildings, etc. Usually, illegal to conduct business out of, unless zoning allows for the dual purpose.

COMMERCIAL PROPERTY – any properties used to conduct business from. Could include various types of industrial, commercial, retail, flex space (office and warehouse), outdoor storage, office, etc. Usually illegal to occupy for living conditions unless zoned for the dual purpose.

PROPERTY VALUE – the amount the property can be sold for at any given time. Most accurate value is only upon a sale, however multiple ways to determine an estimated value for properties include appraisals, calculating out comparable through databases of other comparable sold properties, and reviewing current existing properties for sale.

Lease 2 Own

Credit Report mid-FICO's:
Employer:
Job Description:
Current Gross Income:
Years Employed by Current Employer:
Date Verified Employment:

# of Type of Account on Joint/Individual Credit Report
# of Positive Accounts:
# of Derogatory Accounts:
# of Public Records (see attached and notes below):
# of Credit Reports ordered in prior 12 months:

Investors Purchase Price plus Closing Costs:
Maximum Approved ML2O Buyer's Purchase Price:

Debt-To-Income Ratios:

Current Rent or Estimated Principle and Interest
Mortgage Insurance Premium for FHA
Property Taxes
Owner's Insurance
Home Owners Association Fees
Long-Term Debt (Monthly Minimum Payments)

Total Considered Debt:

Source of and Proof of Funds:

Estimated # of Months for Buyers to get Financing:

Notes and Special Areas of Concern:

My Lease 2 Own Notes:

Review by Mortgage Advisor:

My Lease 2 Own Buyer	My Lease 2 Own Buyer	My Lease 2 Own Buyer
Robert Smith	Susan Smith	
664	658	
NV Energy	not working at this time	
Quality Manager		
$9,167		
zero years, two months		
Joint	Joint	
38		
15		
One: CH7BK DISCH. 09-11		
6		
$183,000	Current Interest Rate: 3.75%	
$201,300	Added 1.5% to Int. Rate: 5.25%	

Current	My Lease 2 Own	Future (Purchase)
25%	36%	29%
$1,600	$2,114	$1,122
		$330
$0	$201	$201
$0	$50	$50
$0	$300	$300
$673	$673	$673
$2,273	$3,338	$2,676

Wells Fargo Bank Statements ending Aug. 31, 2012

12

Borrowers have no current rent or mortgage. They recently sold their home in Yorba Linda, CA and are now living in Reno at Extended Stay Hotel until they find a suitable home to purchase or Lease to own. BK Discharge papers do not look complete, I only received four pages of Summary from CA BK Court. I suggest a request of the complete BK papers. Also, Income taxes have not been presented. What I did receive is the E-File Signature authorization with summary information for 2010 and 2011 and W-2's for both years. I suggest request of complete tax returns for 2010 and 2011.

The Smiths look like good LTO candidates. Mrs. Smith is a school teacher and she will look for work in Reno once they have established a home residence so more household income to follow.

Peter Padilla	**Date:** September 20, 2012
at Summit Funding	**Referring Realtor:** Steve Sixberry

Address:	1024 Haywood
ROI Strategies' Equity:	$39,300
Gross Rent / Year:	$17,556
Net Cash Flow / Year:	$7,265
Cash on Cash Return / Year:	18.5%
IRR upon Sale Year 5:	17.8%

Sample of an individual home owned as a Lease 2 Own with our group of investors.

Address:	1955 Sierra Oaks
ROI Strategies' Equity:	$54,600
Gross Rent / Year:	$23,988
Net Cash Flow / Year:	$10,323
Cash on Cash Return / Year:	18.9%
IRR upon Sale Year 5:	11.6%

Sample of an individual home owned as a Lease 2 Own with our group of investors.

Address:	957 Spanish Springs
ROI Strategies' Equity:	$22,800
Gross Rent / Year:	$12,804
Net Cash Flow / Year:	$5,061
Cash on Cash Return / Year:	22.2%
IRR upon Sale Year 5:	23.6%

Sample of an individual home owned as a Lease 2 Own with our group of investors.

Address:	17705 Fairfax Ct
ROI Strategies' Equity:	$32,200
Gross Rent / Year:	$12,144
Net Cash Flow / Year:	$5,600
Cash on Cash Return / Year:	17.4%
IRR upon Sale Year 5:	11.8%

Sample of an individual home owned as a Lease 2 Own with our group of investors.

Address:	7545 Lighthouse
ROI Strategies' Equity:	$47,950
Gross Rent / Year:	$18,084
Net Cash Flow / Year:	$8,673
Cash on Cash Return / Year:	18.1%
IRR upon Sale Year 5:	12.6%

Sample of an individual home owned as a Lease 2 Own with our group of investors.

Address:	951 Sutro Terrace
ROI Strategies' Equity:	$48,600
Gross Rent / Year:	$21,384
Net Cash Flow / Year:	$8,972
Cash on Cash Return / Year:	18.5%
IRR upon Sale Year 5:	11.3%

Sample of an individual home owned as a Lease 2 Own with our group of investors.